D0939467

NATURE NEVER STOPS TALKING

NATURE NEVER STOPS TALKING

THE WONDERFUL INGENUITY OF NATURE

Samuel J. Alibrando

Tsaba House
Reedley, California

Cover design by Bookwrights Design
Interior Design by Pete Masterson, Aeonix Publishing Group
Senior Editor, Jodie Nazaroff
Cover art courtesy Dover Pictorial Archives
Author photo by Andrea Schwagerl

First Edition:

Library of Congress Cataloging-in-Publication

Alibrando, Samuel J.
    Nature never stops talking : the wonderful ingenuity of
        nature / Samuel J. Alibrando.-- 1st ed.
            p. cm.
    ISBN-13: 978-0-9725486-4-9 (pbk. : alk. paper)
    ISBN-10: 0-9725486-4-5 (pbk. : alk. paper)
    1. Natural history. 2. Nature. 3. Science. I. Title.
    QH81.A35 2005
    508--dc22

                                2005010866

Published by:
Tsaba House
2252 12th Street
Reedley, California 93654

Visit our website at: www.TsabaHouse.com

Printed in the United States of America

THANKFUL ACKNOWLEDGEMENTS

If this book brings pleasure or value, I am glad. Join me in crediting others as well. Although we choose which influences will change us and what opportunities to embrace; I must publicly acknowledge some influences and opportunities given to me.

Harry Conn, who has left this world, was a tremendous inspiration to me. In 1972, he told me that I was a "seminal thinker," which I did not even understand. He explained to me that most people have thoughts that are merely a combination of other peoples' ideas. He said a seminal thinker had original thoughts and reasoned from his own thinking. I was incredibly flattered, certain that a tremendous man like Harry Conn would never lower himself to flattering anyone, especially a young (at that time) kid like me. It literally changed my view of myself. He himself was truly a seminal thinker and author. His book does not reflect the full greatness of this man whom I had the privilege to know and love.

I must also thank Murray Norris, also no longer walking among us. In 1979, he strongly encouraged me to write. His ability to alter people's ideas with speaking and writing was wonderful to behold. The world could use more people like Murray Norris. He was an experienced writer and a fast two-finger speed typist. He gave me confidence that what I had to say was important. His insistence that I use my abilities was a great motivation.

The Mountain Press, a relatively small newspaper in the foothills north of Fresno, provided an outlet for my articles from 1994 to 2004. Positive community endorsement spurred personal inspiration in me, enough to continue my ongoing column for ten years. This could have never happened without the Mountain Press first considering my material worthwhile and granting me copyright.

Lastly, I want to thank my publisher, the Tsaba House staff. When a group puts their energy, time, money, alliances, and resources into a focused effort to promote a writer's work it is a terrific affirmation for the author. Thank you for validating and publishing my work.

CONTENTS

BEGINNINGS

PLANTS AND TREES

INSECTS

SPECIFIC CREATURES

DNA

THE HUMAN BODY

YEAH, WHAT ABOUT THAT?

APPENDIX

INTRODUCTION

I have been enjoying writing articles about nature for 10 years in a small, local paper for foothill residents in central California.

For years, even before the column, I enjoyed pointing out certain things to my children (now fully grown) about the clever design of natural things. Most often, I would pull a leaf off a tree and say, "This was an idea before it was created. We can physically touch what was once an idea."

I have also actually been asked if I was a scientist. Ha! In my turbulent youth I ran away from home and dropped out of school. Later I got a GED and went on to college. More than 25 years later I have remained a mere 6 credits shy of even an AA degree.

In my thirties, something sparked a renewed sense of wonder at the marvelous things around me—like trees. I became hungry for understanding more details.

A love for understanding is a quest. It has a different and more rewarding satisfaction than being force-fed education. That is why so many millions continue reading all kinds of books long after they leave school—for pleasure.

Be encouraged. Anyone can grow in knowledge with or without school if he or she has the desire. But I would like to comment on the general attitude in education today.

There really are not many college students who are as hungry for the truth as they are for the good grades. I was the same way in college. I would love to see that change.

It isn't so much the educational system but the larger American culture of "money is success." Almost all students are after the degree NOT education. The degree is simply a means to an end. And what is that end? You already know—a better paying job. Learning has very little to do with motives in going to college.

Colleges, the government and many publications market college degrees in financial terms, the emphasis on the monetary gain, with no mention of the joy of learning. The joy of learning sounds almost frivolous now compared to money.

Today we hear many say they believe graduate students are educated away from their common sense. I think there may be a hair of truth to this.

Many of the more educated tend to lean toward books and experts where those less educated seem to lean more toward their own reasoning.

I think it is a much better student who listens and questions. The questioning student is rare. I am not talking about questioning to get the goods on the upcoming exam. I mean the one who is concerned about the greater test. That is the test of personal satisfaction that what has been learned is actually true. This student doesn't care who said it or what the book says, that doesn't mean it is true until he can understand it. Bravo.

Having been a college student myself, I found that my fellow students were exasperated by my questions to delve into the truth but had no bearing on the exam. So, I know there is even some peer pressure to not pursue the truth.

I say first hear from teachers and books but filter things through what you are sure you already know to be true.

The true student of life is always seeking. Are there inconsistencies? If it doesn't make sense or line up isn't it wrong to not challenge the status quo, the professor or the book?

This is why there may be a widening chasm between the "very educated" and those who rely on their own powers of reason. In the world of Academia, quoting experts is not only acceptable "proof" but also sometimes a way of showing off. You need a good memory to do this, not real knowledge. A computer can "memorize" but humans can truly reason. (I must admit though, I wish I had a better memory).

I think it is a shame when educated people and even educators merely repeat what they have been taught. It is a show of memory, not reasoning. Many cannot answer why they believe what they believe other than to say they agree with the experts. They don't know why they believe because they never asked the hard questions for themselves. If they have a question, they read a book—discussion over.

The word "education" comes from the Latin "e duco" meaning to lead out. This is what education should do. It should lead students above and beyond the masses in both knowledge and greater powers of reason leading to appreciation and understanding.

This is not a book on education but I do feel true education should empower thinkers to transcend previous boundaries.

I encourage people to look at facts. Generally, the nature of people is to be attracted to the truth. Truth is attractive. Let's start with what is true.

Personally, I see hard evidence of intelligence in every tree, every flower, every star, and every single natural thing in the universe.

There is no end to the examples available for this type of column or book. In a world where chaos, inefficiency, disappointment, worry, despair and grief thrive, I have the pleasure of examining then publishing the order, surprising efficiency, marvel, beauty and perfection of things in nature. Sometimes I feel like a kid thrilled with discovery. I love taking a closer look at designs and incredible engineering. Mentally turning over another "rock" in anticipation of what I may find feels like I did as a youngster on Christmas morning. Anybody can do the same.

Does anybody see this contradiction? While multitudes idealize the supreme wisdom of nature they, at the same time, declare it required zero intelligence to design nature, which I find bizarre.

Just as contradictory is the fact that in the industrialized world, man considers himself the ultimate intelligence. Man as the inventor. Man as the conqueror of sea, space and environment. Man the great genius. And I agree. Man certainly is the ultimate intelligence on our planet, hands down. But note the irony in claiming that it took absolutely no intelligence to create something as incredible as man.

THE BOOK

The articles are celebration, not argument. While celebrating, however, there are hints or direct questions. It is my hope this book brings repetitious enjoyment for you and those in your family. A little more biology, physics, chemistry, anatomy, astronomy, and other scientific knowledge are nice by-products—like vitamins in a sweet treat.

You do not need to commit to read the entire book or even read it in sequence. It may actually be more enjoyable to read in small parts. Poke around the table of contents and go right to something that interests you.

Most of what you will read is derived from articles written for a newspaper column. Each article has a beginning and an end. It is the kind of book appropriate for the coffee table, as they say, and there is much to contemplate.

ABOUT THE ARTICLES

Some of the articles were published in the *Mountain Press* in Prather, California off and on since 1994. These articles do not represent all of the articles and are not reprinted in the sequence published. We have taken poetic license to make some minor improvements in hopes of clarifying some vague sentences or correcting grammatical errors. The editors have also made valuable improvements and we have merged some similar topics.

I hope you enjoy reading these articles half as much as I have writing them but my greatest joy was in pondering the ideas expressed.

In addition, there are a significant number of new, never published articles.

THE ADDITIONS —"IN THE KITCHEN"

The articles are like friendly talks "on the porch" with company visiting. Mixed in with these standard articles you will see something that differs from them. I call these other articles "In the Kitchen." We say goodnight to our company and then we go inside to the kitchen where I make some more direct points. These "In the Kitchen" articles have never been published before. They are what I believe to be observed LAWS that I call "Alibrando's Laws." Although there is a list of the Laws numbered 1 through 11, the Laws are interspersed throughout the book to flow with the content of the articles. The first time you read about a Law "in the kitchen" it may be Law #7 and several articles later you may see Law #6.

Secondly, there are "ripples" of laws. These are logical conclusions of a law but a different point that may not be obvious. They seemed too similar to consider a new and separate law. Only Laws 9 and 10 have ripples. I think this will make plainer sense when you read them.

In the back of the book I also have SEVEN RULES that I would love to see practiced in the field of science. There are also a few additional observations.

Ten years ago, when I began writing these articles, there were no "laws" or "rules" in my mind. I merely observed fascinating things to celebrate. However, patterns began to bubble to my consciousness.

It is my love of science that motivates me to address the silliness of the unscientific things parading as science. I love science and it should be clearly separated from theory for everyone, which by the way, I offer as a good idea for a rule.

To some of you, this book will be making a point of something you may already agree with. To others I think it will be very interesting to see the inconsistency of science versus theory quoted as science. The third group that will find this book entertaining are those who are often unaware that some of their own beliefs contradict one another. It is my hope some of you will see this more clearly as you read.

"In The Kitchen" Format

Before you begin reading, I want you to understand the format just for the Alibrando's Laws—*"In the Kitchen"*

I chose to use this format because I want you to understand the need for even stating a law, so I state the "Un-provable Notion" first.

Next I present the "Sensible Fact." However, critics may find flaws in that Sensible Fact so I make a more technical official law statement with the "Technical Wording."

The Technical Wording may at first look like jargon but it is not. It is more like using English to present wording with mathematical accuracy so the phrase itself is more accurate.

After The Technical Wording you will generally find a graphic followed by the explanation and sometimes examples.

Since there are multiple meanings for words, I would like to clarify the distinction in the way I use "Law" as opposed to "Rule":

Law – Activities that have been observed to occur 100% of the time with unvarying uniformity under the same conditions.

Rule – A prescription served as a guide, generally observed in the interest of order.

I hope you, the reader, can enjoy these ideas and have your mind tickled or challenged by all of this. Of course and as always, ponder these things honestly and draw your own conclusions.

Now that you've seen the menu, let's go onto the porch and chat a little.

EARTH AND SPACE

SNOWFLAKES

Snowflakes: there is so much about them that makes us wonder. Sure, we grownups who live in snow country may think of chains for our tires or dangerous road conditions, but if we reflect for a moment, we can remember the romance of snowflakes. The beauty and mystery of billions of silent jewels floating out of the sky gently easing onto the trees, grass, roofs, cars, parking lots and roads is no fairy tale. Without a sound, it seems our world is hushed and cleansed by some magic from heaven. How could it be that each of the billions of six-sided crystals that renew the vast landscape is unique? Each and every snowflake landing on our shoulders, hat, our nose and eyelashes, as far as we can see and for miles beyond our vision, is truly one of a kind. What miracle is this? Instead of cold icicles crashing down on us or spearing us with deadly force, snowflakes descend gently. The snowflakes offer a slight touch across our cheek and behold, the air and sky are filled with them.

The acoustics of a sky filled with feathery flakes creates a sacred quiet. I suppose due to my own memories, the serene quiet that snowflakes create seems so perfect for Christmas carolers, children laughing or just happy voices of friends.

My fascination with snowflakes was renewed when I recently read that they are not white. In fact, they are ice crystals formed from water vapor. The crystalline shape is a product of the below-freezing temperatures that converts the moisture. Once formed, each crystal attracts a microscopic dust or salt particle as its own core. As its descent continues toward earth, it continues attracting more particles enlarging its size and uniqueness. Yielding to gravity, the crystals tumble and fall colliding in space with each other until perhaps a million crystals unite to form the matchless, precious snowflake that lands on your palm and melts in seconds.

Their brilliance surpasses our own vision. As I said, they are not white. Each one contains millions of tiny, clear, light-reactive prisms. Imagine millions of prisms. What a sight to consider. While these prisms break up the light that strikes them into all the colors of the rainbow our own eyes receive a sensory overload; it is too many colors, we are unable to perceive the dazzling display, so our eyes see "white" instead. With all the mystery of such splendor as snowflakes, I learned that we don't see the half of it. The millions of prisms creating millions of colors in each snowflake are too beautiful to even perceive. This is probably my least scientific article when I conclude, based on my emotional perception of beauty, that such beauty is too wonderful to shrug off as an accident. For the moment, I prefer and enjoy being awed.

Sphere of Heights

Like everything else I have investigated, this too turned out to be far more important and far more complex than I originally assumed. I am referring to plain ol' air. The air around us is a much greater gift than I imagined. We have a pretty blue sky and air to breathe, but to have that security while orbiting in cold, black space takes some doing.

We can all figure that there must be layers between us and deep, dark space. However, depending on which field of science is looking at the atmosphere, layers are categorized differently. Some use chemical activity, but the most common is temperature patterns.

A sphere is a round ball. The earth is an imperfect sphere. There are layers around the entire earth like hollow balls with the earth inside. There are six layers named by temperature patterns all ending in "sphere." That is because these layers completely engulf the earth in a sphere-like manner.

Closest to the earth is the TROPOSPHERE (1). This is where all of our weather occurs. It is 6–12 miles thick with the thinner portion at the poles. It gets colder as we go higher. At the top, it is 50 below zero.

At the next level above our Troposphere, is the STRATOSPHERE (2). Here the temperature pattern reverses and it begins getting warmer as we keep floating upward instead of colder. This layer is about 20 miles thick. Jets fly here. Inside the Stratosphere is the ozone layer. When a layer has gases that trap or screen harmful sunrays, it gets hotter as we go higher. Therefore, the Stratosphere heats up to 32 degrees Fahrenheit at the top. 32 degrees may not be too hot but at the bottom, it was 50 below zero. That is a 72-degree increase in those 20 miles.

The spaces between layers have steady temperature and properties; then the temperature patterns reverse at the next layer. At the top of the Troposphere is the TROPOPAUSE layer. At the top of the stratosphere is the STRATOPAUSE layer.

The third layer is the MESOSPHERE (3). "Meso" means middle. Again, the temperature pattern reverses and as we climb it starts getting colder for 20 more miles, until the temperature drops to 148 degrees below zero. Brrrr, that is cold! Obviously, no gases are trapping sunrays here. The top of the mesosphere is approximately 50 miles up from the earth's surface.

After some steady temperature is the THERMOSPHERE (4), much thicker than the lower three layers. This is approximately 230 miles thick and heats up as we continue climbing. It gets hotter and hotter to more than 3,600 degrees. Now we are melting.

Above that furnace is the next blanket; the 280 mile thick EXO-SPHERE (5). Here the air is extremely thin with little gas, so it keeps getting colder again.

The outermost layer is the MAGNETOSPHERE (6) with no gases at all. It was just discovered in the 1960's. See "magnet" in there? This region is where solar winds and earth's magnetic field interact. There are huge electrical currents here. This layer provides an additional barrier stopping many space particles from entering earth's atmosphere. Its thickness changes from the solar winds.

Consider the complexity and patterns of each functional layer constantly reversing temperature properties and ultimately providing an environment on our planet where a delicate flower can sprout and live.

On the internet, there are volumes of research on each of these spheres protecting and providing for our planet. I could do at least an article on each.

We are babes, not yet in kindergarten, as far as what we know about our immediate environment. What a delicately, well thought out design yet powerful enough to protect us so that we are insulated from the harshness of outer space.

So perfect, so complete… and some call it a thoughtless coincidence.

PROTECTING EARTH

Cataclysmic stories and movies are popular. I wonder if the appeal is to something deep inside us that knows we are vulnerable to total destruction that is really beyond our control. Even a slight change, like a few degrees, brings El Nino. Compared to space, a large asteroid is a speck yet it may threaten earth. Earthquakes, epidemics, hurricanes, tornadoes, insect infestation and more natural causes can frighten us—and rightfully so.

But just as awesome, are some of the ways we are protected; our immune system, humanity's amazing survival through the centuries and the way earth is protected from so many dangers that could threaten us from outer space.

Previously, I wrote an article on the various spheres surrounding the earth and their approximate thickness. There were six spheres protecting the earth, but the outermost sphere is the MAGNETOSPHERE. I did not disclose its thickness.

Like a basketball, a sphere is hollow in the middle. Six spheres each outside the other surround our earth. The earth is the little nut inside these spheres, but the MAGNETOSPHERE is actually not round like the rest. It is a magnetic field.

The magnetic field would look like two large grapefruit on two sides of the earth, with the earth the size of a ping-pong ball. One grapefruit is on the sunny side, and the other on the dark side. This is what the MAGNETOSPHERE would look like if it were sitting in space, not influenced or affected by anything else. But our earth *is* affected by the sun. The sun is emitting powerful solar winds filled with dangerous protons and electrons. This is beating on the magnetic field "squashing" it on the sunny side. On the dark side, the magnetic field is being stretched. Another picture for you is water going downstream against a rock. The water compresses on the upstream (sunny) side and the water lines are elongated on the downstream (dark) side.

This field of protection on the squashed sunny side is about 40,000 miles thick. Did you get that? 40,000 miles! The dark, long side is about 1.2 million miles. However, this is not 2-dimensional. It is 3-dimensional if you can imagine this shape. This magnetic shell that is constantly bombarded with supersonic solar wind protects our delicate planet. A shock wave is produced as these supersonic solar winds hit that shell. The solar winds decelerate (slow down) and become much bumpier within the magnetosphere. As they keep penetrating the next five protective spheres, they are warm, life-giving rays of sunshine by the time they reach earth.

Could man design and create such a vast protective system as this? If we lost these spheres, how could we possibly construct these same spheres ourselves? Apparently, if these details were overlooked, it would be total disaster.

FLASH LIGHTNING!
Twister was a movie about the destructive force of violent tornadoes.

Lightning is responsible for 100–200 American fatalities each year and hundreds more injuries; more than hurricanes and tornadoes.

Annual American property loss is SEVERAL HUNDRED MILLION dollars every year. No pyromaniac can compete with lightning. Lightning causes more than 10,000 forest fires a year in the U.S.; that is 27 fires a day!

Only a couple of generations ago, the word "interdependent" was introduced. However, the existence of interdependence began long before any man can know.

"Symbiotic" is an even newer word and as science uncovered more evidence on the vast inter-linking of so many life forms, chemicals and systems, environmental consciousness has emerged.

We continually discover that we know so very little.

What is lightning for?

I would love to hear more about it if any readers know.

Clouds build up positive and negative charges like on a battery. Why they separate is unknown; however, there are some theories. Here are a couple of them:

1. The positive charge goes to the top of the cloud and the negative charge to the bottom. Over one half of all lightning occurs within clouds as they neutralize the recurring separation of charges.

2. About 40% of lightning goes from the clouds to the ground. The lower part of the cloud (negative) is attracted to the positively charged ground.

Typically, within the cloud, the charge (negative) moves downward about 165 feet in microseconds. This aimed collective movement is called a "stepped leader." When the stepped leader reaches 330 feet ANOTHER stepped leader from the ground (positive) moves UP. This especially happens on protruding objects such as trees or buildings. The swift climb of the positive stepped leader meets the descending stepped leader and BAM! The brilliant light we call "lightning."

Several subsequent strokes can follow that same channel in less than a second, until the negative charge center in the cloud is eliminated.

Lightning is a larger than life version of static electricity in your carpet, clothes or hair.

Fascinating, huh? The roar of thunder you hear is the explosive heating and expansion of air.

You can study this further under "electrostatics."

Lightning is huge. It is powerful. It is constant. We don't know much about what would happen to our world if lightening stopped but it is here with all of its properties with millions impressed by its dramatic power.

PUT CLOUDS ON YOUR PLANET

If you ever get to manufacture your own planet somewhere, be sure to have a pretty blue sky. Of course, that could get pretty boring. Why don't you throw in some clouds to continually alter your huge blue, half-dome canvas? This can make for unpredictable sunrises and sunsets much more beautiful than without clouds. Taking in hues and reflecting light, clouds that can still be seen after sunset make a striking contrast against a dark sky.

On your planet, invent properties that create different patterns of clouds. For instance, on our planet we have ten cloud formation families subdivided into three altitude groups. Yeah, our earthly scientists have given them all names and every single one ends with the letters u-s. Like cirrus, cirrocumulus and cirrostratus. Those are three high cloud formations between 16,500 and 45,000 feet.

So how do you plan to make these clouds for your planet? Here, all clouds are just a visible mass of water droplets. Sometimes they are ice crystals, but that is just another form of water. They are often a mixture of ice and water but what makes it a cloud is suspending it in air at a considerable height. If we drop the height to the ground we're just gonna have to call it "fog." Fog is just a cloud low to the ground.

But wait. How do you make separate clouds with all those changing shapes?

When I used to work at Camp Sierra, on particularly hot days it would sometimes briefly rain at the end of the day. It was from all that evaporation in the valley below; those sweating people, the lakes giving up moisture into the air, the trees and plants yielding moisture in that scorching 100-degree weather. The moist air rises. Something you may not know (I didn't) is that as you go to higher elevations there is lower air pressure. This allows for expansion, and not only of potato chip bags that sometimes pop when you go to the mountains but moist air also expands. Are you still with me? The mass of moist air is cooling as it rises until the temperature drops below the "dew point" and becomes supersaturated.

Now we have excess water that will condense onto any microscopic dust or smoke particles it can find. Ta-daaa! Now we have teeny, tiny water droplets about .0004 (four thousandths) of an inch in diameter grouped together making a CLOUD. This is one of those fluffy white clouds, if the sun is shining on it. That would be nice on your planet.

Now all you need is wind in various directions to keep moving and reshaping the clouds. Of course, we haven't figured out how to make wind yet. Hey, while you're at it, make rain clouds too. This way you can salvage all lost moisture and send water all over the world without plumbing.

If your planet ends up anything like ours, you are going to definitely need clouds because most plant life depends on water from rain here. In addition, without rain on our earth, we would have worldwide drought and that would end plant and animal life. Except for humans that figure out an alternate method of getting fresh water from the sea, human life would also perish. Having no rain clouds kinda wrecks the whole planet so I guess the clouds are more than just pretty.

Hey, these are some good ideas for your planet. Just copy the cloud ideas here already on ours.

So who is responsible for the cloud thing here?

How Big Is Big?

Mankind is so brilliant, so wise, and so superior; we have concluded that no greater intelligence could be responsible for our world, its creatures, its plants, ourselves or even earth's suspension in space orbiting around the sun.

Now how can we calculate just how much man and all science knows?

How do we figure what 100% of knowledge is and then calculate what percentage of it we know? Just not knowing the answer to that proves we have no idea of what we do not know.

In terms of plain "bigness," we know that mountains are big and the ocean is bigger. The earth is huge. It is nearly 25,000 miles around. But let's look at measuring space. It can be done three ways. One mile isn't too far going down the road, but one *square* mile is 640 acres. That is 1,760 yards long by 1,760 yards wide. Those 640 acres comes to a total 3,097,600 square yards. Picture a person just standing in every 3 feet by 3 feet square space. That is 3,097,600 people. More than 3 million people could stand on a one square mile parcel of property.

Do you want to guess how many square miles would be required for a world population of 5 billion? I mean, like if they were all attending some big fair, even if we give everyone 25 square feet (5 feet by 5 feet), you would be surprised. You check my numbers—about 68 miles long by 68 miles wide is big enough. That would make about 4,500 square miles.

Now do you begin to see how big a square mile really is? Pretty big!

However, a *cubic* mile is one mile tall, one mile wide, and one mile long. You can hardly imagine how much space this really is.

One cubic yard is like a box that is 3 feet high by 3 feet long by 3 feet wide. The average person could fit into two of those boxes stacked six feet high and 3 feet wide. Remember this in a minute; it takes two cubic yards to fit one person.

Here is an amazing calculation. Do you know how many people could fit into one cubic mile, just standing there in a 3-foot wide box, 6 feet high on top of and next to each other?

Well, one cubic mile has 5,451,776,000 cubic yards to be exact. If we give each person two cubic yards, we could fit the population of the entire planet into just TWO cubic miles. We all need more space to live, but if we were all inside some telephone booth we could all fit in TWO cubic miles while the rest of the planet would be completely absent of all human life. Although we can fit the world population in only two cubic miles, the earth itself has nearly 260 cubic miles. No, that's not right; 260,000— no 260,000,000—no. Our earth ball has 260 *billion* (260,000,000,000) cubic miles. We've got some room here, especially if we start digging. If we need only 2 cubic miles to fit everyone on the planet and there are 260,000,000 cubic miles in earth alone—that's plenty of space.

Earth is big but not compared to Jupiter, Neptune, Uranus and Saturn.

Uranus, ("yurinis." the "polite" pronunciation) takes eighty-four of our years to make one trip around the sun way out there in its own much wider orbit. The planet Uranus has a 32,500-mile diameter through its middle, compared to earth's nearly 8,000-mile diameter. It would only be about four times the size of earth if it was only wider but of course, it is a ball, not a saucer. We are talking cubic again. According to the '94 Microsoft Encarta encyclopedia, it is *sixty-seven times the size of earth.* We decided earth was big—but Uranus is sixty-seven times bigger!

Neptune is bigger still. It is seventy-two times larger than our entire planet.

Saturn, the one with the rings around it, is even bigger than Neptune.

Jupiter is the granddaddy of our solar system and is more than *one thousand* times the size of earth; man, that is gargantuan—huge—gigantic!

You could take 1,400 planet earths and stick them into a ball the size of Jupiter.

Of course, the sun is bigger than the planets that orbit around it; you could put 1.3 million earths inside a ball as big as the sun. The earth seems to be shrinking, huh?

The sun, which is 1.3 million times larger than the earth, is just a medium-sized star about 9,300 degrees Fahrenheit on the surface, which seems hot enough. However, the temperature is about 29,000,000 degrees in the middle of the sun.

So, what percent of all this space does man think he has mastered? Does he understand what he sees? Does he understand what keeps the planets spinning? Does he know why the planets orbit counter-clockwise instead of clockwise? Does he know why some moons go in opposite directions on other planets? Does he know why the sun itself revolves every 27 days? Can we make our own miniature solar system that is more accurate than any clock? Can we then make that man-made miniature solar system float in the air, orbit around a center ball with mini-orbits of moons and satellites around the orbiting planets?

Does man even comprehend his own sky—how his own clouds are made—how to make rain—how to stop the ocean waves on the shoreline? Does he understand even how his own body works, grows, heals and ages? Do individuals even understand their own behavior, why they think what they think and how their emotions interact with relationships?

What percentage of all knowledge does man really have, 50%, 10%, 1%, or some tiny fraction of one percent? We don't even know.

Yet, we still have the gall to shake our fist at the very notion of any greater intelligence than ourselves.

Amazing!

SOLAR SYSTEM

With Jupiter being 1,400 times the size of earth, we know there are some huge planets rotating in space. Our sun is 1.3 million times the size of earth. However, this sun and planets are dwarfed by the size of the solar system of which they are members. The farthest planet, Pluto, has been re-categorized as *not* a planet but it is more than 32 billion miles from the sun. We could draw a line from Pluto's orbit to the sun to make a radius measuring the solar system. The radius is 3½ billion miles, so the diameter is 7 billion miles. There is a span about 7 billion miles wide and almost 22 billion miles around the outside of this circle, the circumference. Within the circle are 38 billion square miles, but this is still only our solar system within our own personal galaxy, which is larger still.

Our sun is a star. Our sun is merely one of hundreds of millions of stars orbiting around a common center. Our particular galaxy is called the Milky Way.

Things are now getting so big astronomers have created and use measurements other than "miles" to measure great distances.

For instance, from the earth to the sun is about 93 million miles. Astronomers use that as a yardstick and call it an "AU" (Astronomical Unit). So it is simply one AU from earth to the sun. Our 7 billion-mile wide solar system is about 75 AU's broad.

Now our 75 AU solar system is actually just a small part of our own Milky Way galaxy. We need even bigger measures.

You have heard of "light years." One "light year" is almost 8 trillion miles. That is an unwieldy number. It is so big.

206,265 AU's or 19 trillion miles, is a distance they call a "Parsec." Now it is almost getting ridiculous.

1 AU = 93 MILLION MILES

1 LIGHT YEAR = UNDER 8 TRILLION MILES

1 PARSEC = 206,265 AU's = 19 TRILLION MILES

Okay, is parsec something you can understand? Do you really understand how far a one million mile trip is? Well, driving at 60 MPH 24 hours a day would take nearly 2 years to travel a million miles. In a supersonic jet at 600 MPH, it would take nearly 2½ months. Now if I make a quantum leap with that supersonic jet and fly 24 hours a day at 600 MPH to cross a parsec, it would take more than 3½ million years. Yeah, a parsec is big.

Our Milky Way is about 30,000 parsecs wide. Therefore, that is 30,000 times 19 trillion miles.

I am not even going to try to make such vastness graphic in miles or square feet. But remember, a yard is 3 feet long and our galaxy is 30,000 parsecs.

A *square* yard is not 3, but 9 square feet. Our galaxy in *square* parsecs would be 900,000,000 square parsecs if on one flat surface. However, our galaxy is not a flat pancake but 3-dimensional. It is a sphere.

A *cubic* yard is not 9, but 27 cubic feet. Our galaxy measured as a ball with a 30,000-parsec diameter would be about 14 TRILLION CUBIC PARSECs. It is almost inconceivable.

Wanna figure how many square yards that would be? Not me!

Suddenly our huge sun shrinks to a speck of dust in comparison to the size of our galaxy.

That's just our own galaxy. Astronomers now know of at least 1,900 additional galaxies, with the largest known galaxy having approximately 13 times as many stars as the Milky Way.

Incredibly, our own 14 trillion cubic parsec galaxy even seems to get smaller among so many other galaxies with great distances between each of them.

Our galaxy is dwarfed by the space we know about. Our own galaxy dwarfs our huge solar system. Our solar system dwarfs our sun. The sun dwarfs our earth. Our biggest mountains are dwarfed by the size of the earth. We stand in awe of a huge mountain reaching into the cold atmosphere while its base is enjoying the summer.

Still, mankind, particularly the majority of scientists, is sure that no great intelligence or power greater than us has done this. Accidents, luck, chance... and we know our scientists are too confident in these theories for us to question their conclusions.

Consider this: Even though we can't explore the depths of our own planet beyond 10 miles because the intense heat melts everything, even diamonds, scientists tell us conclusively how our huge universe came into being.

Actually, they do argue about different theories of how our universe has come into existence but a surprising majority insists that if they are sure of one thing, it is this: it was not created—it happened on its own. How do they know that, especially with all they admittedly do not know?

Our scientists theorize and tell us what happened *billions of years* ago and accuse challengers of being ignorant. Many scientists call challengers ignorant, not because the scientists have proof, but because they have spent so much time and money on their theories. Scientists theorize on what is happening *billions of miles* away and billions of years ago, while we do not even know what creatures lurk in our deepest ocean or even twenty miles below the surface of the earth.

For man to be so self-assured that his intelligence is above any other greater intelligence is astronomical ego.

SCIENTIFIC PROPERTIES

WATER LOGIC

The world has mostly ocean on the surface. There are also vast desert regions. Mankind has developed dams, canals, and plumbing to get desired water from one place to another. Underground plumbing is a little like water tables (lakes underground). Canals are like our own rivers and streams. Of course, reservoirs formed by dams are simply man-made lakes. Sure, why not copy simple, good ideas. But how do we bring water to the entire earth? That would take far too much pipe or cement using the manmade methods.

I was studying to get my water operator's certification and the book describes something called the "Hydrologic Cycle." This cycle explains how the earth is watered. It's pretty simple, really. The oceans are constantly evaporating moisture into the air, forming clouds. The wind blows the clouds over dry land and they drop water (rain or snow) as they go. This process conveniently removes the salt from the water. This water fills lakes, rivers and streams or turns into snow and rests on mountaintops. The snow acts as a type of water storage by delaying its feed into the lakes and rivers. The rain clouds water the plants, forests, grasslands and jungles while the deserts don't get much rain. No pipes—no electricity—no cement—no human management.

Rain percolates, like water does through coffee, until it finds a water table. It is called a table because if you could see the outline of the underwater lake from both the top and sides it may remind you of an odd-shaped tabletop. Of course, these underground lakes have their own streams running this way and that but much of the water that does not dissolve into the soil will eventually head back to sea.

Interestingly, the water underground is generally purer, cleaner, safer water than the surface streams and lakes because of the filtering process of passing through dirt. It's funny how dirt *cleans* the water! Ah, this is

another good idea being copied by human technology. Most water fil-
ters have sand and rocks inside of tanks to clean the water so it is pure,
clean and safe to drink.

Naturally, the rivers and streams head back to the sea where the cycle
started. What a great way to water the earth. We save big on plumbing,
dam construction and manufactured canals. It is "Air delivery" of water
via clouds, while simultaneously de-salting, that waters the entire planet.
The deserts, without water, are like spots on your lawn that the sprinkler
doesn't reach. The deserts have their own special critters that survive
with very little moisture.

Economical, simple and incredibly important to all life on the earth,
precious water is delivered without the help of man. How lucky for us (this
is sarcasm) this system was never designed, but like every other incredible thing on earth, it is the result of accidental events.

My study book calls it "Hydrologic Cycle." "Hydro" means water and
"logic" is "science investigating governing principles." That is a paraphrase
of the dictionary definition. "Governing principles" does not strike me
as random accidents. There is logic and reason to all of nature. There are
countless wonderful governing principles keeping us and all life protected and flourishing.

Aero-Dynamics
(Two birds talking)

*"Hey Louie, do you understand how drag and lift work in aerodynam-
ics?"*

"No Frank. Why?"

*"Well, since we're birds and not as smart as people, how come we have
been flying for thousands of years longer than they have?"*

"Gee Frank, I thought you knew."

When the Wright brothers made international news and history with
their famous flight of 120 feet in 1903, it was all over in 12 seconds.

Back in 1903, birds were already a little further along in time and distance of flight than 12 seconds and 120 feet.

The design of any flying bird efficiently utilizes the principles of
flight, gravity and aerodynamics. Additionally, they have such superior
maneuvering capability they can zoom in under one branch and on top
of another, perch and then take off in almost any direction.

I may understand some of the principles of aerodynamics but not well
enough to fly, and certainly not well enough to build a plane. I know I

don't understand it well enough to design a flying machine from my personal familiarity with principles of weight, speed, resistance, lift, drag, air pressure, compensating for shifting winds and turbulence, safe landings—and who knows what else I would need to know.

So how did the birds do it so long ago?

How can they be flying without the input of man's "superior" knowledge?

Besides thousands of species of birds that fly, there are thousands of insect species that fly too. If man couldn't fly until 1903, who fixed the bugs and birds before then?

What? Oh, so that's how they did it.

The scientific community explains it something like this: *There was an explosion billions of years ago and things kept "evolving" and mysteriously cells, genes or DNA coding figured out, billions of years before man did, all the laws of aerodynamics. All this successful designing was then coded in for reproduction. Instinct was added to save time on pilot's training for the birds and bugs.*

Surprisingly we are told this was all quite by accident. Good thing too, because for a minute there it looked like somebody was smarter than us.

"I have a problem with that 'acidental theory,' Frank."

"Yeah, me too, Louie, but hey, we're just birds."

THINGS NOT PHYSICAL

It is always a happy discovery to find a word someone invents that describes something you want to explain. Today I present a fancy word, *"noumenon."* This refers to something beyond sensual grasp—beyond physical perception. It can be observed only by intellectual thought. This would be the opposite of *"phenomenon,"* which is physically observable.

Stay with me and you will see something interesting. Science recognizes all phenomena as something to be studied as truth. No doubt, what really is there—is true. But science neglects something else that is really there. What about all the things that are not physical? We can observe the brain and even deduce electrical impulses as thoughts. However, we cannot see those thoughts. The content of thoughts is not observable in a physical way.

We all have imaginations, but no one's imagination can be put under a microscope. We have regrets, but these too, cannot be chemically broken down.

So, a *noumenal* idea is thinkable but just not knowable by the five senses.

Most misunderstanding of science is not by scientists but by professionals and nonprofessionals that want to make their own points by quoting science. Many teachers, lecturers and writers idealize science as all knowing and never mistaken. Real scientists know the extreme limits of science today. Not only are there many phenomena science cannot explain, there is much it cannot even observe.

When your pet dies, physically and chemically everything is there that was there one minute before, when it lived. What is that essence of life that vanished?

What is it on the inside of us that craves understanding of truth that is of no concern to the animal kingdom? What chemical or cell came into existence to make us think, wonder and pursue answers to questions like; "Who am I? Why am I here? What is love? Is there a God? How can I know I am doing the right thing? What is truth? Is my life fulfilling? Am I attractive? What will happen to me when I die? How big is the universe? and, Where did our world come from?"

What could accidentally spark an inner quest for truth into existence? Can science isolate a chemical and inject it into a horse who suddenly now wants answers to these questions? We cannot find curiosity and put it into a test tube. Ironically, many scientists will declare their pure pursuit of truth with a conviction that if it cannot be tested it may not exist. The most inspired scientists are usually the most curious. Ask those scientists where their curiosity comes from. What does it look like under a microscope? How much does it weigh? What elements together form curiosity? The irony is that the very common denominator that makes great scientists is also something that physical science cannot even analyze—CURIOSITY.

It is a stranger idea that these noumenal things once did not exist in simple life forms and then, by random biological/chemical accident, they appeared and now reside in every human being. How can physical stuff create nonphysical things?

I see no evidence of something lesser creating something greater. Even scientists must admit their curiosity and many other things are not physically observable.

FIRE

We marvel at biological organisms and their intricately superior engineering. We gasp in wonder at the largeness of space and its cosmic orbital consistency to the millisecond. The atmosphere, seasons, animal instinct, the mind of man, reproductive processes of plants and trees worldwide and more—it's all astounding.

However, behind all the "inventions" of nature lie not only scientific principles such as physics, aerodynamics and gravity, but things far more basic like dirt, wind and fire.

Fire was not invented by a caveman or French scientists. I know of no theory that it evolved from a simpler chemical until one day the right chemicals and processes finally figured out how to become fire.

The science of fire is something offered to firefighters all over the country. For years, a triangle was presented as a picture of the necessary parts of fire. Those three sides represented "heat," "fuel," and "oxygen." This way a firefighter knew if he could remove any one of these three, the fire would automatically go out. A propane fire can be stopped by eliminating the *fuel*—propane. A fire in a trash can be put out by putting a lid on it, thus removing the *oxygen*. And if *heat* can be removed or sufficiently lowered, the fire will give up also. Sometimes the mere spray of a firefighters hose can reduce the temperature enough to put out a fire.

In recent years, a fourth side has been added; actually, a bottom to a three-dimensional pyramid. This newer side represents "chemical chain reaction." There are certain chemicals that when combined will ignite into flames and/or explosions. Scientists have learned that the key to these reactions are atoms interacting. Therefore, they have introduced several chemical inhibitors that slow, interrupt or stop these dangerous chemical interactions.

It is fascinating how many different properties fire has. There are both complete and incomplete combustion. There is the threat of heat radiation, smoke and toxic by-products. All these are factored into the strategy of fighting fires.

You see, fire is not a simple thing. I was amazed as a volunteer firefighter, to learn there were 10 different chemical reactions involved to create a "simple" flame. You can research this yourself since it would be too involved to explain the steps. Not that I could explain it without a book in front of me. Just for a quick look, I will tell you a flame involves various reactions and interactions working from the bottom up. Of course, you need the fuel, heat and oxygen but as described in my studying, it includes more. There are atoms and radicals from fragmented molecules. Molecular structures are broken down and radicals forming with other atoms create new compounds. Heat releases more atoms, molecules and radicals. These events draw more oxygen and other atoms into the process. Heat and light are produced. Certain molecules are more diffi-cult to ignite than others, so they wait for greater heat. At the top of the process is smoke.

All this is involved in a single flame. It is very complex and I am sure there are still more scientists that do not know about the parts, proper-ties and behavior of fire.

Although fire can consume tons of materials in minutes like a hun-gry monster, it warms us, cooks our food and provides combustion for all types of engines. It also cleanses and sterilizes. From the sun, it makes life possible on earth. It is a powerful thing that no man can take credit for inventing and as far as I know, has no primitive ancestors.

Every Time You See Ice

We are made up of water more than anything else.

Scientists figure if they find water on another planet, they will also find life on that same planet.

Water is key to all life as we know it. It is obviously a liquid that can freeze into a solid or be heated into a vapor of steam. Few of us know the real properties of liquids. Scientists have gone to the trouble of carefully evaluating precise responses of liquids to temperature.

"Specific heat" is a term used for the specific rate at which liquids conform to temperature. Some liquids heat up quickly to boiling and cool quickly to freezing, like mercury. Of all the liquids, water takes the longest time to heat up and cool down. This is critical to life forms in water. When the air temperature suddenly changes the water of a lake, ocean or stream changes much more gradually. Kinda lucky that water has those properties, huh?

Another principle studied in liquids is how they freeze. The colder liquid gets, the denser it becomes. That means the same weight of liq-uid takes less space as it gets cooler. This is why brake fluid, coolant or transmission fluid in your car have hot and cold levels. When fluids are hot, the measuring gauge shows a higher notch. This is because liquids expand when heated. There is more space in between the molecules. Of course, when the liquid is cold it is denser. It actually takes up less space. Not true with water bottles. Freezing can pop the caps from the water expanding.

Now I am setting this up so pay attention. Every liquid in its frozen form is HEAVIER than in its liquid form. With this in mind, ice cubes should sink to the bottom of every glass and pitcher of water. They don't.

You know ice cubes always float. Water is the only exception to this liquid rule. Other liquids freeze from the bottom up. It's funny how this most important, life-giving liquid (water) has different properties than all other liquids.

I bet you are assuming this water's exception to other liquids has beneficial effects. And why do you assume that? Because you have learned that the more we research nature, the more we discover overwhelming details that mean life when a slight difference would mean death, sometimes to an entire species. We don't expect to find stupid ideas in nature. We expect to find greater and greater engineering. And why? Because nature's design is so perfect, precise and unbelievably connected to dozens, hundreds or thousands of other life systems.

That is why we want to protect nature because we know the wisdom is so much greater than our own.

Like all liquids, water gets denser as it gets colder but then, a strange and unique peculiarity occurs at precisely 4 degrees above freezing, it suddenly gets *LESS* dense. Since it gets less dense only at 33, 34, 35 and 36 degrees Fahrenheit, when it freezes at 32 degrees, it is LESS dense than water and so it floats. So who cares, what's the difference?

If water did not have this particular quality, much of life as we know it would be destroyed. Many other things would also be much different. You see, if ice was *heavier* than water, no one could have ever skated on a frozen lake unless it was 100% frozen. The ice would first form on the bottom of the lake. The lake would freeze from the bottom up. The water on top would become increasingly shallow until we would be able to see the dead, starved fish in the remaining shallow water. All the vegetation at the bottom of the lake would be cut off from the fish by the ice forming from the bottom up.

Do you see how incredibly important it is that water does not conform to the properties of all other liquids?

Remember the exceptional life-preserving property of water every time you see ice floating in your glass.

IT'S NOT EASY KEEPING THINGS ORGANIZED

You know putting water on your fire can put it out. Suppose someone else told you water would heat up your fire. What would you think? On a cold night when your woodstove wasn't quite hot enough, would you try to increase the temperature by throwing a pot of water on your fire? Of course not, that would be dumb, you already know that.

You know it would be dumb because you understand the difference between a "theory" and a "law." Somebody's idea is just a theory until it can be proven.

Whenever anyone tells you their ideas, you should compare it to real facts.

Simple enough; but watch now.

There is a principle law in thermodynamics called "entropy." It is not a theory, but a law. It can be proven. (This won't get heavy. I'll show you).

Entropy states simply that every physical thing known to mankind seems to break down on its own with time. When things get old, they break down; your skin, your clothes, your car, your house, the trees, the stars—everything. This breaking down is considered moving from an orderly state to a more simplified state. Your house, pets, and trees will likely all be dust in 1000 years. You observe this every day.

Entropy is a law.

Evolution is a theory.

Contrary to provable *laws* of physics, specifically entropy, evolution says if you give the dust long enough, it will figure out a way to organize and build itself up.

Let's take a ten-acre cornfield. Suppose a farmer works hard to plant all those straight rows of corn, all ten acres. He dies. The family loses the farm. The bank doesn't sell it; it just sits there. Next year, there is corn but it's all messy. The year after that there are corn and weeds and it doesn't even look like rows anymore. In ten years there will be nothing even looking like orderly rows. That is normal entropy, going from an orderly state to a more simplified state.

The theory of evolution says without a farmer that field may be a mess, but give it long enough and the weeds will leave and the corn will figure out how to get itself organized into ten acres of rows.

Now I ask you, does that make sense to you?

In The Kitchen
Alibrando's Law #7
Time & Deterioration

Un-provable Notion: The more time given, the greater the likelihood of unsupervised organizing (removing flaws, improving capabilities) and expanding a larger, complex interdependent network.

Sensible Fact: The longer anything goes without maintenance, the worse it gets.

TECHNICAL WORDING: *The more time needed to accomplish design accidentally, the greater the likelihood of failure.*

Below, the graphic represents progressions that are equal. An increase in disorder comes naturally with the increase of time (without intelligent maintenance or energy).

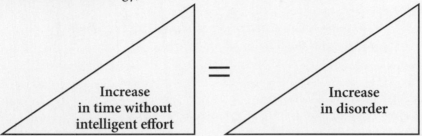

EXPLAINING THE LAW:

All things tend to gravitate to a simpler state—ultimately dust. Your house in 10,000 years, or even you in 10,000 years, will be dust. The ultimate physical destiny of all unattended systems is a de-systemizing to a simpler and simpler state.

It is a scientific principle that all physical things change from ordered and complex to less ordered and more simple. It is like "de-evolution." This is parallel to the 2nd Law of Thermodynamics (you can study this on your own). This means the more years that pass, the greater the deterioration.

This is important because it means any theory claiming that MORE TIME is needed to allow anything to organize itself into greater order without intelligence or supervision is directly contradicting this law.

Do you realize how huge this is?

It is common knowledge that there are far less species on earth than there once were. Many animals today are on the endangered list. The world is not producing new species but reducing the number of species.

This lines up with the idea that systems are losing ground, not growing in organization.

To make a statement like "Over billions and billions of years great organization is possible accidentally" is directly opposing scientific knowledge and law and your common sense.

However, what is provable today is this: The greater the amount of time, the less likely the chance of spontaneous organization. We can prove that with anything, seven days a week. Let that sink in.

A rephrase of this same idea could be: The more time goes by, the more stuff breaks down.

WHEN there is no intentional, intelligent energy input, things go downhill on their own—period.

I hope you can appreciate the impact of this law:

LAW #7
The more time needed to accomplish design accidentally, the greater the likelihood of failure.

RELATED ARTICLES:
It's Not Easy Keeping Things Organized
If We Evolve, Why Can't Cars?

THE SMALL STUFF

LOVE-STARVED AMOEBA

My dog whines at the glass door sometimes. She seems to want attention. It also appears she enjoys and even craves affection. She definitely doesn't like it when I scold her.

From an impersonal rock to single-celled organisms to fish to who knows what, where and why did a craving for attention and affection get put into the evolutionary DNA strands?

I know my dog isn't the only one wanting affection. I also know there are plenty of other animals the same way. We certainly know that people crave attention and affection. I do.

This is a human characteristic, not something unique.

Can the impersonal give rise to personal, design personal or create the personal? Can inanimate objects invent and organize emotions?

Cats purr. People get flattered or respond in kind. A smile and a polite hello or a Merry Christmas spreads positive feelings. How did this ever come from an amoeba?

After all, the theory goes that all life forms came from non-living chemicals and then BOOM!—the first single-celled organism. Without any intelligent assistance, life began evolving *by accident* into the amazing universe, world, plant, marine, bird, insect, animal and human life we now analyze.

My dog whines. Now how or why would something impersonal mutate into something personal? How could something like the "need for affection" be invented by something impersonal? Think about that. Anyway, it seems more like a flaw than an evolutionary step up when it comes to survival. After all, how does loneliness help anyone? I am sure there would be millions of gallons of alcohol NOT sold each year if there was no such thing as loneliness. Was emotion invented for the purpose of bonding and reproduction? You don't need loneliness for that. Hormones seem to work well enough for reproduction.

The need for affection and positive attention is universal. It is literally vital to human infants. It is so vital that infants can die without affection—literally.

This has also been proven experimentally with baby monkeys. The poor little guys are fed and provided with a healthy environment, but no touch. They die.

They also have experimented with baby monkeys to see whether they would prefer the metal screen wire mesh version the size and shape of a mommy with artificial eyes and mouth and most importantly—a milk bottle. The other mommy had no milk bottle or food, but was a cuddly, fuzzy monkey doll of the same size as the metal mommy. Guess what? The baby monkey preferred cuddly mommy without food to a cold, metal mommy offering the provision of food.

This is not true for molds, fungus or paramecium. This need is not for reproduction. Maybe it's for safety, so the youngster stays close to mama? My dog is well past needing her mama and she still whines for affection; sometimes so do I. Many songs through generations have been about the need to be loved.

Still, the larger question looms scientifically, "How could a simple life form or even a bug come up with the idea of "need for affection" and then have it originate not only in itself but insert that characteristic into its DNA for all future generations?

Unlikely?—more like impossible. You tell me how it is possible and I will consider it. Meanwhile, I will stick to the principle that where there is intelligent design there is intelligence.

Consistent with that pattern would be this: where there is the invention of "need for affection" is an inventor who already has that need or at least the capability of experiencing it. Still others think the opposite, even though we all need affection.

MAKING A CELL SMELL & TELL

Imagine the unlikelihood of the very first cell that can smell. It doesn't necessarily have a nose but can detect an odor. Suddenly, aromas that were never detectable by anything anywhere on the planet were being smelled for the very first time. Was it a lone cell with an extra sense known by no other living thing?

Now hold on; a cell that can only smell has no advantage because it has to send the information to the brain for any smell to mean anything at all. Then the brain needs to receive that information and interpret it. What good is information if it means nothing?

Anyway, one cell is not going to help much. We need way more cells than one to make a critter able to smell. And then we need to link smart instincts with those smells so it is useful to the creature. The critter should be able to know this smell is food, that smell is toxic, this smell means nothing, that smell means danger and so forth.

How does one invent a cell that can smell in the first place? Technically, it is called an olfactory cell. What exactly gives a cell the ability to detect odor?

A dog has so many olfactory cells it can smell things we wouldn't dream of smelling. My dog likes to stick her head out the window to smell things as we drive. She loves it. You've seen dogs stick their noses in the air to get a better whiff.

Obviously, a critter would need far more than one cell in order to actually be able to smell, so the question becomes "How does a network of cells accidentally stumble upon such coordinated ability all at the same time with these new abilities?"

By network, I do not mean dozens, but thousands, tens of thousands or millions of identical olfactory (smelling) cells created all at once and functioning in coordinated unison. And to even make any difference to the critter it must also be plugged into the brain somehow sending signals regarding those scents. The critter must have a program of not only what scents are, but also what to do after smelling those scents. Our newly gifted creature needs automatic understanding for this new smelling ability so he responds correctly to different smells. The critter must also have a "software" program of instincts so this new smelling ability can benefit him. He must know how to react to the different smells such as:

Female in heat—go get her.

This food is rotten—do not eat it.

There is something to eat close by—go find it.

Predator approaching—run away now.

If the program has any errors, it could be big trouble. In other words, instead of being an advantage it could be a disadvantage to have the ability to smell if the meaning of the smells were misinterpreted as in the following examples:

This is rotten—*eat it.*

Predator approaching—*go find it.*

Female in heat—*run away now.*

There is just very little room for error when a sense of smell is first introduced. Otherwise, it could be fatal rather than helpful, and therefore threatening to the species continued existence. Anything less than a perfect understanding accompanying the new ability to smell would be a disadvantage. So it seems the brand-new ability to smell would have to appear as a complete package deal instantly—and only a flawless package.

How does one put all this together all at once in the first creature that can smell? How does DNA gather and program external information outside itself, like the scent of a dangerous predator that is a completely different species, without previous knowledge of that scent and what it represents? Consider how impossible this is then multiply it by every species that can smell.

Every mammal we know of today can smell. Some reptiles smell through their tongues. Some insects smell with their antennae.

Humans are spending millions on aromatherapy, mouthwash and deodorant. Smells are a big part of our lives.

Personally, I love the smell of fresh-baked bread, garlic in the kitchen, and coffee in the morning.

The idea that the ability to smell happened by accident, all at once, with signals to the brain and the correct instincts for reaction is … a little hard to believe. Then take that entire perfect package of smelling, signaling the brain, accurate instincts in response to smells; and plug it into the DNA so that it passes these newly invented abilities into reproduction. How do you program the new invention of identical olfactory cells, signaling hardware and software, instincts and the correct instinct responses from the brain into the DNA so that it also passes on to all the descendents— permanently? By accident?! Hard to swallow?—you betcha!

But wait, we still have to spread this "sense of smell" into almost all the creatures on the planet. The same smell is a friend to one species and an enemy to another. Every species needs its own special program.

We have to modify the instincts for every different species that has different enemies and eats different foods. DNA must take these "perfect packages" and lock it in forevermore but only AFTER it is perfected.

So all this we call a spontaneous accident…? Well sorry, but that just stinks.

ATOMS—WAY, WAY SMALLER THAN CELLS

Our bodies are made up of mostly water. Obviously, we are more complex than a puddle of water. Various cells bring organization to our body. We have specific cells for fingernails, different cells for eyeballs, heart tissue, bone, blood and so on. Makes me feel like I am in some alien movie when I am made up of all individual living things that do their own thing to survive and function. When we examine cells we discover organisms that need nutrition, reproduce, live and die. There are different characteristics to cell types but all are functional, organized systems. Atoms are more than 1,000 times smaller than a cell. They have a nucleus (center) and electrons.

This is like a completely new universe of principles, properties and realities. Each atom is like a miniature solar system with its center (the nucleus) having distant electrons orbiting. Instead of the electrons circling around in the same place it may circle once sideways, then next time overhead and under and the next time a little above sideways. The electron orbits at all angles around the nucleus but it does maintain a relatively consistent distance. If we lit an electron and took a time-exposed photograph, it would look like a distant ball or shell around the nucleus.

Fascinating, but it's just the beginning. If an atom has three electrons, only the first two electrons will be in the inner orbit. The third electron will circle the nucleus outside the inner two. As a matter of fact, and I do mean *fact*, the inner two will share the same orbit "shell." How do I know this? I know this because *all* atoms but one have two electrons in their inner shell—no exceptions. The *one* atom that has only one electron, my friend, would be the hydrogen atom. You see, the precise number of atoms determines exactly what the element will be. Two electrons make it a helium atom. Three electrons make it lithium.

Atoms are the building blocks of literally every single thing in the universe. Cells, viruses, caterpillars, pelicans, mountains, oceans, air, stars, planets, fire, lawnmowers, light bulbs, laser beams, air, snow, DNA… EVERYTHING!

The electron orbits have a very specific pattern, too. Each electron orbit path or "shell" has a consistently specific maximum for all atoms. The second orbit or "shell" has a maximum of eight electrons—NEVER more than eight. It can have less than eight but not more. Therefore, if an atom has twelve electrons, we know the first shell (orbit) has a maximum of two and the second orbital shell has eight (that is ten so far) and the remaining two electrons will "spill over" into the third and most exterior shell (orbit).

Science actually knows that the structure of each orbit has a consistent maximum. Every atom in the universe has a maximum of seven shells. You do understand that the reason I keep using the word shell is because the orbit does not stay on the same two-dimensional plane but keeps circling at different angles forming more of a shell or sphere rather than a circle. Each shell has a maximum number of electrons. From the inside to the furthest outside shell, it goes like this:

> First shell (inside) = 2 maximum electrons
> Second shell = 8 maximum electrons
> Third shell = 18 maximum electrons
> Forth shell = 32 maximum electrons
> Fifth shell = 21 maximum electrons
> Sixth shell = 9 maximum electrons
> Seventh shell (outside) = 2 maximum electrons

That is the exact sequence of maximum electrons per shell in every atom in the universe. However, most elements and atoms do not use all seven shells.

The most complex naturally occurring atom structure, using all the maximums comes to ninety-two electrons and that is uranium.

Atoms have no DNA. They are much, much smaller than DNA. DNA is made up of atoms. Since we cannot credit DNA for the design and organization of atoms, who or what designed the atom?

How Much Difference Can One Electron Make?
Do you have any idea how small an electron is?

In another article, I mentioned atoms are about 1,000 times smaller than cells.

The atom is mostly space. Obviously, the nucleus of the atom is far smaller than the circle of the orbiting electrons. The nucleus in proportion to the whole atom size is like a marble sitting inside a huge ball with a diameter as big as a football field. Remember, it is the whole atom that is 1,000 times smaller than a cell.

An electron itself is about $1/1000^{th}$ the size of the atom nucleus. I am not saying an electron is $1/1000^{th}$ the size of the atom but just $1/1000^{th}$ the size of the atom nucleus.

Imagine some bug 1,000 times smaller than a marble flying 100-yards away (91 meters) in circles around a marble that is floating in space. That tiny bug is flying above it, below it, and to the right and left as it continually orbits around that marble. This would be similar to an electron orbiting the nucleus of an atom.

There are internet sites that say it is not 100 yards away but ½ mile away.

The sizes are not exactly equivalent in all elements but you get a little bit of a feel for how tiny an electron is. It is so small… we still have not invented the technology to physically see an electron.

Still, electrons are big time technology on a very small scale. How much of a difference can one minute electron make to the tiny atom or the world?

There is something strange about atoms. Depending on the number of electrons, they are stable or unstable. I will tell you some stable numbers but first let me say that if they are unstable they "look" to hook up with another atom to "steal" or share an electron to get to that stable number of electrons.

What makes this even more significant is that as soon as an atom has any change in the number of electrons it becomes a different element; even if it's only one more or one less electron.

Yeah, no metamorphosis in a cocoon, just BAM! It's instantly another element. And if that changes several times in a second it is literally several elements during that second.

Now, here are the rules; *unchangeable* rules.

1 electron = Hydrogen	5 electrons = Boron
2 electrons = Helium	6 electrons = Carbon
3 electrons = Lithium	7 electrons = Nitrogen
4 electrons = Beryllium	8 electrons = Oxygen.

Those are the rules, no exceptions. 1 electron = Hydrogen. It cannot be any other element, hybrid or mutation of anything, it is *only* and *always* Hydrogen.

There are ninety naturally occurring atoms and scientists have managed to make about twenty-five more.

That is what one teeny, tiny, small, currently impossible to see electron can do.

It can completely change the element and is why 79 electrons make gold, 47 make silver, and 92 make uranium.

Now a "stable atom" is one that has completely filled an orbit with the maximum number of electrons. Maximum is like a table designed to sit on a certain number of legs. For example, let's say eight. The table is unstable with one to seven legs and considered stable only when it has all eight legs.

As stated in *Atoms–Way, Way Smaller Than Cells,* an atom can have up to seven orbits each with its own unique number of maximum electrons. Some scientists have done an awful lot of work to learn all this without even being able to see these little electron guys. Let's look at the exact number of maximum electrons per orbit from the innermost to the outermost orbit throughout the universe once again:

First orbit, 2

Second orbit, 8

Third orbit, 18

Fourth orbit, 32

Fifth orbit, 21

Sixth orbit, 9

Seventh orbit, 2

I hope that you said "Aha! They are not all unique, the first and seventh orbit each have two." Okay, Okay, you're right.

Are you getting the feeling stuff not only looks organized but exact math formulas under gird everything, precisely dictating what is what? There is nothing random about atoms or electrons. I used to say the staggering odds of a "simple" one-celled life form spontaneously being created were zero. How can there be such a thing as a "simple life form" if there is no such thing as a simple atom? The more I learn it becomes more and more evident that just one atom being accidentally constructed would be pretty impossible. Especially if you add that once perfectly established, it will forever have exact, universal, unchangeable rules for every atom in the universe obeying the same laws.

Although there is much known about the *behavior* of electrons, no one knows what electrons are made of or what they look like. However, we know they are precise, abide by laws, and that they make up literally everything known to man.

Lucky for us, atoms are accidentally holding our universe together.

Gee, what are the odds of that?

In The Kitchen

Alibrando's Law #6
Random Rule

Un-provable Notion: Random, unintentional occurrences have accidentally designed everything on earth and in the universe that is not man-made.

Sensible Fact: "Random" is contradictory to "designed."

Technical Wording: *When something is random, it is not designed. When something is designed, it is not random.*

Random ≠ Designed

EXPLAINING THE LAW:

Anything designed is not random, but designed. Anything random is random and therefore not designed. Nothing can be both. They are by definition, opposites.

The phrase "Random Design" is in itself a contradiction in terms.

The meaning of "design" contradicts and is the opposite of "random."

A truly random event is a completely unguided, unmotivated, unplanned, no agenda occurrence, correctly synonymous with "accident."

"Design" involves choice, intention and effort while "random" is the absence of choice, intention and effort.

If a carjacker has an "accident" with another car in order to steal it... guess what? It is not really an accident.

What confuses us more is when we hear things about the evolution of all life being random but sometimes hear it is also somehow guided internally by some "power of nature" or some undefined instinct.

Well, is it random or guided? It cannot be random AND guided.

If we agree it is guided, then we can begin investigating the "guiding power" if the scientist is not saying he really believes it is random.

If the theories suggest any type of guidance, it would be plainer for them to say, "Although it appears random, it seems to be guided by powerful forces in nature."

LAW #6

When something is random, it is not designed. When something is designed, it is not random.

RELATED ARTICLES:
Overload
Way Smaller than Cells
Most of the articles in this book

BEGINNINGS

SIMPLE LIFEFORMS?

Remember the ol' teaching in biology books, "At first there were just simple life forms on the earth."

Of course, this is AFTER the big explosion creating our planet and putting it in orbit in a very orderly solar system with movements now predictable by astronomers forward or backward 1,000 years to the minute.

Simple solar system—gee, is there such a thing as a simple solar system? Before there were any "simple" life forms there was the "simple universe," as though the real beginning of complexity came with the first living thing. Moving on...

How does non-living material spontaneously create a "simple life form"?

If it is so easy for life to appear from electricity and chemicals, should not scientists expect life forms to eventually appear on the moon and all the planets in our solar system? You know, nothing spectacular just "simple life forms."

A simple life form has to have a few "simple" things to be a living organism.

1. The ability to grow
2. The ability to get food
3. The ability to ingest food
4. The ability to process food
5. The ability to reproduce

Besides having these basic characteristics, there has to be something close by that is also alive for the organism to "capture," eat and digest for its entire lifetime in order for it to survive—food!

Think about that. We cannot have a single "simple life form" all by itself because food also has to be living. Therefore, we need "spontaneous life" to occur at the same time, in the same place with reproductive abilities and living food. A single "simple" life form could not survive unless a previous "simple" life form was already there reproducing as a lifetime supply of food.

Although biological science has advanced in learning how to manipulate DNA, tissue and molecules… science still cannot create or manufacture a living thing from non-living material.

Chemically, scientists can put together proteins and other elements—but they do not live, so they do not function.

So the next time you hear the term "simple life form" as though it is no big deal, could happen anywhere and requires no explanation, ask, "If all of science can't make a simple life form, just how simple is it?"

BIOLOGICAL CLOCKS

I always cracked up at folks using their "official photo" from 10–15 years earlier. When you meet them in person they almost look sick compared to their picture.

After several people mentioned that the photograph next to my column in the local newspaper didn't really look my age at that time, I decided to change it. You know, the older the photo, the younger the face.

Something I find very interesting is the way all of us look a certain age. We all pass through similar physical stages.

We were made the same way and began growing inside of our mothers all the same way. In our 2nd month of life, 7 months before we were even born, we developed these little tooth buds way up near our cheeks.

None of us were born with a big old toothy smile—lucky for nursing mothers too. Our teeth did not push through our gums for many months AFTER we were born.

All of us have some kind of biological clock that is ticking away.

We see babies and try to guess their age.

On the school ground, we can see the second graders are bigger than the first graders.

The dentist will tell you that kids all start with a set of 20 teeth. You know, we call them baby teeth. With all the sugar we gobbled and mud pies we ate, we are fortunate to have all received a second set of teeth, now numbering 32.

It is no accident that we have larger teeth and more of them because our jaw keeps growing. If our 32 teeth were the same size as our baby teeth we would look like a piranha fish with sharp tiny teeth.

There aren't many third grade boys who shave because they are all on the same "clock."

None of us waited until we were 14 before we started growing teeth.

Pimples are bad enough; toothless would have been real tough in junior high.

"Gee, you look like you're not a day over 40!" That's a complement to a 60-year-old but not a 35-year-old. Some people age more gracefully than others but none of those young-looking 65-year olds look 20.

There is some kind of biological clock boundary common in all of us.

Where is this clock and how does it work? Maybe it is the solution to the quest for the fountain of youth. Could we slow the process of aging? Could we speed up or slow down the development of teeth? How does this "clock" stay so coordinated with the whole of the human race, generally?

It is truly amazing, precisely engineered and once again beyond the grasp of all of modern science.

GROWTH GUNK

How do we take some material and make it so THERE IS MORE there on Tuesday than there was on Monday? Not stretched, not inflated, but really more.

Wow, if we can do this, think of the other uses it could have! Let's name it "GROWTH GUNK."

Here is our commercial:

> *Hey, do you spend a fortune on buying new clothes for your growing children? Put GROWTH GUNK in the wash and watch everything grow: socks, underwear, pants, and shirts. That's not all. Put it on hats, belts, and expensive sporting goods: bow and arrows, ice and roller skates, skateboards, baseball gloves, hockey sticks and whatever you need bigger. Got a big family and a small car? Just add "GROWTH GUNK." Now there's room for everybody.*

Why not paint it on your walls? Your ceilings would be higher. Paint the floor to enlarge your square footage.

Science has come a long way in the past fifty years. Computers that once filled a room can now be held in our hand, TVs are both smaller and bigger. There is so much technology today that didn't exist fifty years ago that anyone from that era would have great difficulty even believing it was possible if they hadn't seen it happen. Weather satellites, laser surgery, space shuttles, microwaves, guided missiles, test-tube babies and the list could go on for pages. Ten years from now, things I haven't even dreamed of could be considered common.

We start believing scientists can do anything. But guess what? They can't make a tree. They can't make a flower. They can't even make a single seed … and they can't make stuff grow.

That is not bad news. It leaves lots of room for wonder and poetry. They can't make anything grow that isn't already growing.

And you thought they could do anything. Ha.

Millions of dollars are earned annually just so women can make their eyelashes look maybe a 16th of an inch longer.

How does hair know how long is long enough on certain dogs and cats? Thank goodness, my eyebrows "know" when to *stop* growing.

Everybody hates mowing the lawn but we still want that green grass to grow. This makes not one, but two multi-million dollar industries—one industry to promote the growth of grass and another to trim it.

You see, science can help things grow but it has never manufactured a thing that truly grows itself. Like a 12-foot hose that can grow to 20 feet the following spring.

Remember the one about the boy who wrote his mom and told her he grew a foot at camp; and she starting knitting more socks?

THE FIRST—A CELEBRATION

On January first I thought, "Ah, a New Year; the first day of the first month of the New Year." New beginnings are always exciting. As I was looking around at the thickness of pine trees around me, something occurred to me. Like me, these trees had ancestors. The manzanitas also have ancestors. Here was the revelation, "there had to be a first." That is, a first pine tree or a first manzanita.

No matter what lived before the pine tree, there had to be a pine tree just like the ones I am looking at now. Ancestors… this tree came from that tree which came from that tree, etc.

At a specific place and a specific time, there had to be a *first* pine tree in order for it to reproduce the other pine trees. A tree with a unique DNA set, so that it could be said, "There has never been a tree like this ever before."

There are many pine tree varieties and experts give them each a name, usually Latin. So the pine trees I am looking at have a Latin name, I assume. However, this very specific pine tree came from the pollen of another tree which came from the pollen of another tree … You get the idea. But I repeat, in an exact location, at a specific moment in time, there was the very first original of this particular species, the granddaddy of them all. There is no other logical conclusion.

It would be ridiculous to say that these pine trees have always existed.

It would be silly to say they came from outer space. But even if they did come from outer space, there still would have to be the very first pine tree of this species that reproduced reproducing pine trees. You do see the logic in this, I hope.

We cannot say that the first pine tree was different. That is not what I am talking about. Today, if we found a different pine tree it would be given a *different* name because it would be a *different variety* of pine tree. That different specific variety had to have also had the very first of its kind at a specific point in time in an exact location. From that time and place, it reproduced. The existence of entire forests of any species is evidence of the success of the reproduction and survival of that very first pine tree.

That is exciting to me. The same goes for the manzanita shrub. Way back at a specific point in time, there was the very first manzanita shrub. The fact that I can see and touch a manzanita today is the evidence that there was a first manzanita shrub of this identical species; the *Original Manzanita*, the prototype, the forerunner, not of a variation of what I see and touch, but the exact species of Manzanita that reproduced what is now before me.

If you park your car tonight and tomorrow, find a big dent on the hood, what kind of person would tell you, "It must have always been there"? There was a specific place and time that the dent appeared. It's the same with a tree.

Celebrate the first this year, knowing it is a time of new beginnings and join me in revering that every living thing had its beginning.

In The Kitchen
Alibrando's Law #1
Original Beginnings

UN-PROVABLE NOTION: Things originated *gradually* over billions of years.

SENSIBLE FACT: Every species started specifically, with a very first one.

Technical Wording: *To exist, a thing must first begin, specifically.*

The arrow below represents a specific beginning.

Start of species

→

EXPLAINING THE LAW:

Typically, every species we hear about came from a different ancestor. Of course, we hear that those ancestors came from other species and on and on all the way back to our so-called mutual ancestor, some single-celled living organism that was the first life here on earth. There is tremendous vagueness to specific events that happen over billions and billions of years. It sort of gives license to "anything can happen" over such a vast amount of time. It removes scientific accountability. It removes the *specifics* of any event.

The fact that Law #1 is true without exception demands accountability for how things occur—where, when, how? Every event must be specific, and occur at a specific time whether it is thousands, millions or billions of years between events. This applies to every atom, cell, bug, fish, bird and mammal. Real things happen in real time. We can mark the minute of a birth and the time of death. We can analyze a creature's DNA and determine the exact number of chromosomes. In all the readings of the early stages of evolution, they have always avoided *specific* occurrences with a virtual wave of the hand saying "over billions of years" anything is possible. Are we ignoring the specifics of how things happen? The discoveries are specific, not general. Science always progresses by building on a *specific* basis, usually one experiment or discovery at a time.

The car you drive didn't always exist. It was designed and possibly a prototype was made. If they skipped the prototype and went straight to the assembly line there was THE FIRST MODEL off the assembly line; after that the second and so forth.

Maybe it is a model that has been modified since the 1960's. Even so, this modified, particular model also had an original first as did the previous versions.

Do you have an oak tree in your back yard? There are various species of oak trees but yours is a particular species and it reproduces trees ONLY of the same species. It came from another tree which came from another tree all the way back to THE VERY FIRST OAK TREE of that particular species.

That very first oak tree of the same species (like the one in your back yard) was in this country or a particular part of the world, but most certainly in a *specific* field or on a *specific* mountain, in an *exact* spot. Yep, the very first tree had to be rooted in a specific spot at a particular time. And before that, before the first Oak tree like the one in your back yard, it did not exist… and then there was the very FIRST, a specific and real occurrence in a real world.

You see that squirrel scurry across your lawn. The same applies to it. Although there are various species, the one in your yard is of one specific species and mates accordingly to continue the species. But once upon a time it did not exist and then there was the very first squirrel with the DNA chromosomes and characteristics of this very particular species. Like the tree, it didn't happen *generally* in time and space, but instead it was in a specific region and actually in a particular spot at a very exact time. It didn't exist before that time but it has existed ever since that time. The squirrel scurrying across your lawn is physical proof that what I am saying is true.

There is no other logical sequence of events. Even if there was a different "modified" or more primitive type of squirrel that looked different and somehow mutated, it doesn't change my point here. That primitive ancestor would also have to have a first. The ancestor can be before the new squirrel species but of course, there still has to be an original, very first squirrel that is the same species as the one running your lawn. The first one successfully survived and reproduced and … there's the proof that you can see with your own eyes.

The exact same logic applies to any critter or single-celled organism on the planet. *To exist, they must first begin.*

Every single thing manufactured by man and nature had a FIRST one before it had a second, third and so forth.

I have used many words to describe what should be common sense, but common sense is often lost in ideas presenting themselves as "over your head." In reality, it is "over your head" because it makes no sense. It doesn't work in my head either.

LAW #1
To exist, a thing must first begin, specifically.

RELATED ARTICLES:
The Original Cause

THE "FIRST" HAD TO BE TWO

No matter what you believe about the origin of life, there are certain logical things that are inescapable:

1. Things exist.
2. Things came from somewhere.
3. There had to be a first one of everything.
4. (We will discuss now)

Number four has to do with creatures that have two genders, a mommy and daddy. No matter what you think a cow came from, at sometime in real history there was a bull and cow together to make the first calf.

The very first cow that ever was… are you picturing the first cow? Now imagine the very first cow… without a bull. This is an amazing thought alone. Most importantly, the very first cow (as we know cows today) that ever existed would have quickly vanished if there were only ONE. A single cow all by itself, no matter how much grass was around could only live and die and that would be the end of cows. Why? Because without baby cows, cows cease to exist. No more cows!

Whether the first cow arrived suddenly or gradually, all the cows we see today are evidence that there was once a first cow AND AT THE SAME TIME AND PLACE the very first bull with the same number of chromosomes, that grazes, that moos, that has horns, etc.

The very first cow that ever was, HAD TO HAVE AN ENCOUNTER WITH THE FIRST BULL, otherwise—certain extinction…

The same logic applies on the flip side. You could not have bulls for hundreds, thousands or millions of years and then have the first female bull (cow) finally evolve from them. Bulls (as we know them) cannot have baby bulls without a cow. To say they can—that's bull!

Cows and bulls are a two-gender (boy-girl) kind of animal. The very first cow and bull could not live 3,000 miles from each other and make babies. They couldn't have lived a hundred years apart and produce babies. The very first cow and bull had to be alive at the same time close enough to get together and have calves. That's plenty close!

So not just "once upon a time" but in a very specific place on a certain day, the very first cow and bull appeared and not only lived, but had the incredible ability to reproduce by coming together. Not only did they have the ability to make "babies" but also for good reason, without a trainer or manual, they knew how. From their action came the very first calf from the very first bull and cow.

It is challenging enough to ponder the wonder of any *very first* crea-
ture coming into existence with such incredibly sophisticated engineer-
ing that all of science cannot even copy it; but with two-gender species,
THERE ALWAYS HAD TO BE TWO AT THE SAME TIME AND
PLACE. Every single creature (species) that has male and female, HAD
TO HAVE BOTH (male and female) EXISTING TOGETHER, FROM
THE BEGINNING OF ITS EXISTENCE.

Number Four: The origin of every two-sex species (male and female)
had to have a very first male and a very first female simultaneously, in
the same place, in order to perpetuate a species.

There was no first squirrel, there had to be a first male squirrel and a
first female squirrel, *together.* It's the same for all mammals, birds, most
fish, lots of bugs, some trees (ginkgo trees are male and female, bi-gen-
der) and whatever else takes two. This would be true for humans too. A
very first man and woman (as we know them today) first appeared at the
same time and place. Like the old song, "It Takes Two, Baby."

Think of the incredible repercussions of what I am telling you. Every
single two-gender species that exists today is evidence that all of them,
without exception, instantaneously and simultaneously appeared in male
& female form at the same location with the ability and instinct to reproduce. Any other notion is completely illogical.

Tell me again, it is not by design.

IN THE KITCHEN
Alibrando's Law #2
Paired Origins
UN-PROVABLE NOTION: A new male and female species emerges accidentally.

SENSIBLE FACT: New species requiring male/female reproduction cannot continue without a new species mate.

TECHNICAL WORDING: *All new species requiring two genders to reproduce must have both MALE and FEMALE emerge into existence at the
same time, AND in the same location, AND with the instinct and ability
to reproduce.*

The simple graphic below represents male and female type species needing to be present together to continue as a species.

Male + Female ━━━━━━━━━━━━━━━━━━━━━➤   SPECIES

EXPLAINING THE LAW:
How many species exist today that cannot reproduce without a mate?

If this law is true, and it is, then every "accident" to bring every single one of those "I need a mate to reproduce" species has to occur in TWOs. Not just twos but perfectly matched twos of male and female in the same location at the same time.

My Parents Were Not Like Me—An Unlikely Story
If you believe a different theory, we need to imagine the specifics of how this different theory works. Imagine the very first raccoon being the very first of its kind. This means a couple things. One, its parents were not raccoons, at least not like this new, first raccoon. Two, its parents are a different species. Do you understand for it to be a new species it must literally be a different species that never existed before. It had to be born a new species. It couldn't be born the same species as its parents and then later in life change and become a different species.

A different species means they have a different number of chromosomes. The parents have a different number of chromosomes because they are a different species giving birth to a brand new creature. The brand new raccoon can never reproduce with its parents' species. Hmmm, if it is a male raccoon with a unique number of chromosomes how can it ever reproduce? Its kind never existed before. It can't just go and reproduce with any other animal on the planet. It can only reproduce with one of its own to survive as this new species. Since it just "evolved" and was just born and is unique throughout the world, where can it find a mate? If it finds no mate, the first of its kind will also be the last.

Well, there are only two possibilities for finding a mate. But before I say what they are, consider the slim odds of any mother and father of one species having a baby that is a completely different species; not only a completely different species, but an *improved* species (according to one theory). Consider all the known scientific laws this violates. We know today that DNA is militant in making sure species reproduce only their own, and if there is any dramatic deviation, the offspring are sterile. This is a type of "quality control" built into and carried out by the DNA.

Therefore, for the unlikely theory to work, the mother must have both male and female new creature babies that match so that they are able to reproduce with each other. The litter, or pair, has to all be the new, evolved species of raccoon. That seems easier to swallow than the second possibility of a close neighbor accidentally and coincidentally having an identical match for the new raccoon.

But we still are not done. This brand new male raccoon and the first ever female raccoon must be attracted to one another so that they do, in fact, mate.

The unlikelihood of the one in a billion chance has just become one in ten billion because one is absolutely not enough. We have to create/evolve/invent the exact same type of species but with opposite sex chromosomes so they can mate.

Unfortunately, we are still not done defying science as we know it. After achieving this masterful, although highly unlikely, feat their babies (the new raccoons) must "lock in" the DNA so they basically stop evolving in order to keep reproducing *only* raccoons for many generations. We have raccoons today and guess what they have for babies? Yep, raccoons—and only raccoons of the identical species; this is what we see in all DNA today in every single species. This is so the species is maintained and NOT CHANGED. So, to change a species, we have to overcome the policing action of DNA that *prevents* the change of the species and after we change it, we have to allow DNA to resume its authority and quality control again to protect the new species.

Is this getting complicated? You betcha! The further we walk away from what is sensible, the more complicated it gets. It is not sophisticated science, it is anti-science.

It is so unlike anything we know to be true and so statistically improbable; and we are only describing ONE new species. We are taught to believe that this is how every single species on the planet came into existence, from parents that were another species. Every species of insect, fish, bird, reptile, mammal and even some trees trace back to some great granddaddy single-cell that was parent to a different kind of cell and eventually became the proud grandparents of maybe a jellyfish who had descendents that were not jellyfish but fish . . .

You know the story, but have you ever been taught to think about the specifics of making this work?

I didn't think so.

No matter what, we should be able to at least universally agree on this point:

LAW #2

All new species requiring two genders to reproduce must have both MALE and FEMALE emerge into existence at the same time, AND in the same location, AND with instinct and ability to reproduce.

RELATED ARTICLES:
The First Had to Be Two

UNIVERSAL TIME & SEASONS

There was a popular song in the 60's by the Byrd's, "Turn, Turn, Turn" from the Bible.

"To every thing there is a season, and a time to every purpose under the heaven:"

Something I enjoy here in the California foothills is all the wildflowers that blossom in April. The yellow, white and purple flowers are picturesque to see as painted dabs on mountains; or as delicate, individual jewels of beauty close-up.

In August, they are gone, but then these taller yellow flowers are still blossoming along my driveway.

In September, we always hear the buzz of meat bees both close and in the distance.

If I kept a diary of when certain things happen, I would learn much more about nature's clock through almost everything around me.

We have summer, autumn, winter, and spring. In the lower hemisphere (south of the equator), they have their winter in June, July, and August and their summer from December to March.

You can practically set your watch to blossoms, leaves changing colors, mating seasons, migrations, certain species' birth cycles, hibernations and many more things of which I have yet to learn.

The moon, sun, and planets are not in the living organism category, however, they also keep incredible and predictable accuracy.

The earth takes, what we call, 24 hours to rotate once all the way around. It travels in an oblong path around the sun and comes back to the same place after doing this 365 and ¼ times (our "year"). To make up for that ¼ day we have leap year every four years and just add a "day."

Astronomers know the timing of orbits, eclipses, comets and other space activity with such precision that many events are predicted hundreds of years before they actually occur. They love the time and math demonstrated in the universe.

In 1955, the International Astronomical Union defined the time frame of a "second" as being 1/31,556,925.9747 of the solar year in progress at noon on December 31, 1899. Then the International Committee on Weights and Measures later adopted that same definition in 1956.

Manmade science has been sloppy and erroneous for thousands of years but the more we learn, the more design and exactitude in timing we discover in nature and space.

Biologically, terms of pregnancy are predictable due to the design of the species. "Pre-mature" signifies *before* the time we now recognize and accept that it should have been.

Professional fishermen learn much about migrations of schools of some species of fish.

Farmers understand the timing in regard to planting and harvesting and anticipate when to expect an onslaught of certain pests.

Zoologists and Veterinarians have so much more to learn than human doctors because each species has different systems, designs, clocks and unique features.

Humans, as well as creatures, have "clocks" for when certain stages kick in. Babies have "clocks" for teeth, walking, talking, puberty, hormones, change of life and so on. You talk to any specialist in any field—dentist, surgeon, pediatrician, eye doctor, etc.—and they should be able to inform you about some additional aspect of your own body's clock in their given field.

Worldwide, all creatures, plants, stars, moons and planets have all these amazing layers of incredible timing that work in sync with so many untold numbers of living and non-living things… together… predictable… and very well. How could such vast, synchronized choreography have been designed except under management?

OVERLOAD

I can actually appreciate the idea that all things in nature just happened by accident. It's called "overload."

Consider even one tree and how there is such massive industry within that tree. Every cell has a job and every cell gets "paid" what it needs to live and thrive. Within every tree are coordinated efforts on a grand scale utilizing resources outside itself. It is harvesting nutrients from the soil while leaves draw from the sun. The chlorophyll in every leaf is busy executing photosynthesis and manufacturing food daily. That food is delivered to the leaves, limbs, trunk, and cells and to every extremity of the tree through the canals (also built intelligently). None of this would be possible for the chlorophyll without the sun or water. Depending on the size of the tree, we are talking millions or billions of cells without a leader functioning together with the common cause of the health of the entirety, which in this case is a tree. What a flawless society. If attacked by insects other cells trigger chemical warfare to either sterilize, mildly poison or attack the nervous system of the insects, and science has learned the tree will even warn other trees (of the same species) of the attack.

I have covered some of these aspects in other articles but my point here is that all of this is just one tree. When you add the earthworms that aerate the soil, the sun that makes photosynthesis possible, the precious oxygen in the atmosphere and in some cases, the insects or wind needed for pollination multiplied by all the forests of the world it becomes overwhelming—all this interdependence… so seamlessly functional.

What about the way rain is brought to the trees by a system that uses evaporated water from the ocean, stores it in a cloud which has no power to transport itself, but is gracefully moved by the wind and then drops the water in areas so consistently that weathermen report "average rainfalls" for every region? Add to this all the vegetation on the planet and all the mammals and all the fish and all the birds and all the insects and the properties of atmosphere, wind, seasons, sun and moon, the solar system and our to-the-second consistent orbit around the sun. Take all of that, coordinated, in harmony and interdependent like the tree with cells performing various tasks while thriving in its environment utilizing vital resources outside itself—it is so huge.

As we examine further we find that the organization goes even beyond the cellular level to a sub-atomic level. It becomes overload. It is incomprehensible how all this could be so incredibly organized, so what do we conclude? Since it is too much for us to understand, it must be an accident. It is so intelligent that it seems beyond intelligence so it must be from no intelligence; which, by the way, I think is about the most unintelligent conclusion one could make.

THE ORIGINAL CAUSE—A MIND BLOWER

Like most children, I would look up at the stars and wonder just how far it was to the edge of the universe. Then I would wonder what the end of the universe was made of. Was it hard? Was it smooth? What was it made of? How thick was it? And of course, what was on the other side? Naturally, I considered if there was something on the other side of the end of the universe, then it really wasn't the end after all. Just about then, my brain would start short-circuiting and I would have to think about something else.

In a similar fashion, the beginning of things is mind-boggling. Before the earth, what? Before the universe, what? What caused the universe to come into existence? Whatever that thing was, how did it come about? Whatever was before our universe that caused our universe to come into existence… how did it get here and what caused that to come into existence?

These are not just philosophical questions they are math questions. Obviously, when light travels into space, we want to measure how far it goes before it hits the end or whatever it does.

I am certain of one thing; our brain is limited. It is not infinite, it is finite. Our brain does not go on forever like space but has a beginning and an end—a limit. Logically, we must calculate that infinity exists. Have I lost you?

A brain like ours cannot comprehend infinity but we can certainly deduce that it exists. It is a logical conclusion. Space has no end. Even if it is a circle, something must be outside that circle. Even if there is a wall at the "end," that wall either has something on the other side of it, or that wall is infinitely thick and goes on forever. This refers to space. From what I just discussed, we can only logically conclude that space must be infinite. We cannot comprehend infinity with our finite (limited) mind but we can deduce its existence.

I am discussing space pertaining to how large space can be. But what about the other way, how small is final? Does smallness stop at some point?

How small can we go? Once cells were discovered, all of science considered them the smallest things in existence. Later we learned cells had many parts. Eventually atoms were discovered but we found that even atoms have different kinds of elements in their make-up. Guess what? We are not exactly sure what those elements are made from. With all the infinity before us, after us and around us and maybe even in us, we sure are a tiny slice of space.

What about time? Once we go back to the "beginning" what was before that and for how long? Does your brain hurt yet? We can only end up concluding time as infinite because we cannot make any sense of time not existing before the so-called beginning. Okay, let your brain take in some oxygen.

Likewise, the very first *thing* had to come from somewhere. What was before anything? Okay, I am going to show you the only possible logical conclusions. It must be only one of two possibilities:

1. There are an infinite number of causes (always something else before something else forever and ever).

2. The first cause is infinite (one infinite first cause before everything else)

If we conclude that infinity must exist in regard to sources where anything comes from and we go backwards to infinity, then we can only conclude one of these two possibilities for infinity.

Okay, so space must be infinite, time must be infinite and the source of all things must be infinite.

Now here is the funny part. It is downright comical that the notion taught in most universities around the world is that we know in all infinity that there is no one smarter than humankind is today.

Most universities teach "we are the supreme intelligence, so if we didn't create infinite space, infinite time, or infinite sources and since mankind did not fill all those dimensions of infinity with precise order, then it must have happened by accident."

How ignorant and conceited is that? Does that sound even logical to you?

With all that we do not know, with all the superior design in us, around us and beyond us—and then to say there is no greater intelligence than man… it forces me to add another dimension of infinity— "infinite arrogance."

PLANTS AND TREES

WHAT IS GENIUS COMPARED TO A TULIP?

What is the definition of genius? Is it a mastermind, great intellect, outstanding ability or abnormally high talent? And in what categories do we recognize genius; Frank Lloyd Wright in architecture and design, Leonardo da Vinci in art and invention? Engineering, biology, science, botany and astronomy, all have their geniuses.

I went to Monterey and Carmel and saw some of the most beautiful scenery in the world. However, at one restaurant, every table had a simple tulip. My wife showed it to me. Inside, there were six little stems or stamen. Each tip was triangular, but also the six tips were arranged forming one triangle. Like most of nature, everything was symmetrical. However, the red tulip on the inside had a purplish bottom shaped like a clover. What a contrast with the bright yellow stamen against the deep purple inside a red tulip. It was simply beautiful. This was not just artistry. Although its days are numbered, this thing is alive. It is the descendent of who knows how many generations of tulips, a distinct flower with characteristics unique to the tulip. It is not nor will it ever be a daisy, a rose or a sunflower. It is a tulip. Its DNA code dictates not only how to survive and reproduce but also how to look; symmetrical, colorful, functional and beautiful. It is genius in every sense of the word—genius in art, genius in engineering, genius in architecture, genius in botany, genius in efficiency, genius in survival. And here it is to hold in my own hand; to touch, to experience like it is no big deal—genius, sheer genius! Genius so great, its wisdom exceeds the reach of all scientific minds. There is no exaggerating here. Plastic flattery is what we make, so you can have a "tulip" that never dies, but the plastic tulip never lives.

I went to Carmel and admired marvelous artwork. Again, artists' homage to the beauty of flowers put on canvass, made in glass, copper, stone, alabaster, wood; in honor of unmatchable genius—unquestionable genius.

That is my point. The wisdom to create a tulip may be *un*attainable but the evidence of its genius is right in front of us. The evidence is close enough for anyone to admire. Like the artist's work is not the bizarre artistic result of error and unguided hands, but careful inspiration coupled with talent. The sheer and utter genius of some talented engineer is not by mistaken design from spilled food on blueprint paper; but rather hard, deliberate work with exact calculations to prove its function on paper before the assembly. The tulip is brilliant excellence universally recognized and copied but never quite matched.

After all, what is genius compared to a tulip?

SPREADING SEEDS

Years ago (around 1994) when I thought I would try writing a column, it was because I was amazed at how many tricky ways seeds spread themselves. I would carefully look at the seeds that stuck to my pants, socks and shoelaces. They are determined little things clinging to my clothes. Some were sticky others had little "jabbers," while still others had little spiral hooks. I have no idea what kind of seed they were, but I was fascinated with the clever simplicity of how they moved themselves without any mobility of their own.

I never could find what I was looking for in this regard through the years, but now I may be on the right path—now that I have the fancy, scientific words for the simple spreading of seeds.

For instance, some seeds are designed so that the wind carries them until they land in a place with the purpose of germinating and taking root. Would you believe there is a word just for the seeds that are spread using the wind? "Anemochory" is the word. It's a weird and difficult word. Most allergies are from pollen in the air. Next time you hear someone sneeze ask if they have an Anemochory problem. Even if you pronounce it wrong, no one will correct you. I can just about guarantee that. I plan to research this whole field (no pun intended) more because, as I previously stated, I am intrigued with how such devices could be dreamed up in the first place.

Apparently, I am not the first curious observer. There is another field of science that researches only seeds that are spread by water called "Hydrochory." Already you should see a pattern and some of you know "hydro" refers to water. It must be pretty vast to get its own scientific word.

I will read up on that too. I will search the internet; I may even try to get the pronunciation.

I suppose the category of seeds that stick on people doesn't have a scientific name. Actually, it does, but it applies to animals. I know how much fun it is to get all those sticky things off dogs too. These types of seeds that spread via animals come under the banner of "Zoochory." That's easy, huh? By now you may have noticed they all end with "c-h-o-r-y" and *zoo*chory is animals.

This realm of scientific study doesn't limit the spread of seeds to wind, water and animals though. Any guesses? How about "Saurochory"? "Sauro," as in "saurus"—it is the spread of seeds by reptiles. I guess there is a lot I don't know about reptiles spreading seeds but I can learn.

Don't quit now, there's "Ornithochory," by birds and "Myrmecochory," by ants and they even break down the animal category three ways. If the diaspores (seeds) are carried inside the animal, it is called "Endozoochory." If it is carried on the outside, like on your pet's fur, it is called "Epizoochory." I suppose the seeds on your sneakers and kids are most accurately described here, as in "Epizoochory." They even have a name if the seed is INTENTIONALLY carried by a creature; mostly in the mouth (birds and ants were cited as examples). That is called "Synzoochory."

I know it is overwhelming, all these weird "chory" words (I don't know if it's pronounced "KORY" or "CHOREY"). When most think of spreading seeds, they think of one of those pushcarts you go over the lawn with. However, what I just described shows that the realm of seed spreading is far vaster and sophisticated than I imagined. I think all scientific researchers discover this too. All the trees, weeds, wildflowers and various plant life spread all over the world without the aid of man. The more you investigate any field of science or any part of anything the layers of design go deeper and deeper until one has to declare, "This can't be an accident!"

IN THE KITCHEN

Alibrando's Law #3
Environmental Inventory

UN-PROVABLE NOTION: AFTER a new species emerges they discover critical resources necessary and *then* evolve accordingly.

SENSIBLE FACT: If you can't live in the environment, you die.

Technical Wording: *A newly emerged species must BEGIN compatible with the environment and already have all the necessary resources to survive.*

The circles below represent how any living species is dependent on things OUTSIDE itself in order to survive.

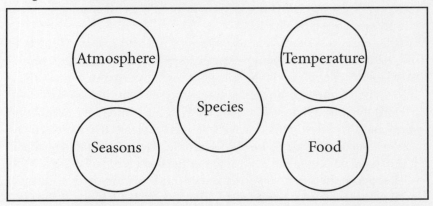

A new species is not here for a short visit but to live here permanently.

If you were moving to Mars permanently, how much would you need to know about Mars before going? How important is it that you don't miscalculate details about what is available there and what you will need to survive in order to live there your whole life?

Explaining the Law:

Dependent: No living thing can provide food for itself from within itself for long.

All life-forms are so dependent they will perish as a species quickly if they do not have everything they need. Things like food, the right temperature range, an environment suitable for its breathing apparatus, etc. are critical for survival. They must survive long enough to reproduce in order to continue as a species.

Specific Inventory of Resources in the Environment: Plants need sun. Aquatic creatures need water. Mammals need oxygen. All of these things are OUTSIDE the creature. Its organs must match the air. Its digestive system must match the available food. Its knowledge must recognize the difference between poison and food, friend and enemy, safety and danger.

Every new living creature's design must involve many decisions regarding camouflage, defense, attacking abilities, hunting abilities, or attracting the yet un-invented mate.

No Room for Error: No life-form can miscalculate what its environment will be; if it designs itself to live in freezing temperatures but is born into a tropical zone—big trouble. If it designs itself to breathe oxygen but is born underwater, it may drown. If a flower needs light and emerges in Alaska for months of darkness—it will die.

It is far too easy to starve or die before reproducing without correct and adequate resources. How lucky would you be to go on an unplanned trip to Mars and just *happen* have absolutely everything you need for yourself, children and grandchildren forever?

Do you see how much this lessens the likelihood of so-called "random design"? There are far too many factors that must be accurately calculated before creating a new species for a specific environment.

An idea can develop and evolve, but for any living thing to literally survive, function and thrive, its whole design must work within whatever environment it will be in right at the start. It must be capable of recognizing and utilizing the resources that are already there. A miscalculation can spell disaster and immediate extinction. On this basis, I would offer for your consideration:

LAW #3

A newly emerged species must BEGIN compatible with the environment and already have all the necessary resources to survive.

RELATED ARTICLES:
Spreading Seeds
Drilling Isn't Always Boring
Dumb Wasps, Smart Orchids
Simple Life-forms
Green?

GREEN?

I was looking at the trees recently and asked myself, "Why green?" It's just a color and I know that chlorophyll inside of plants is green, but why *green*?

When I was a child, we were taught that black absorbed the sunlight more than any other color and white reflected it. Some years back, I heard that the teaching had changed. Now green was considered the most absorbing color. Funny thing is, as a kid, I actually wondered why the plants weren't black if that was the best color for absorbing sunlight. Well, whadya know, green is the right color.

If green is the right color, how many colors do you think the "random process" of evolution had to tinker with before it settled on green?

Maybe dinosaur movies should have blue palm trees, purple fern, and some orange grass. They could tell us the plant kingdom had not evolved to the most suitable green color yet. Sounds silly for some reason, huh? Scary thing is if I said this at a big natural science convention with 160 pages of "research," they would probably take it seriously!

Okay, how's this? All plants, leaves and pine needles mechanizing photosynthesis were mostly green. How's that for a theory? Somewhere, somehow GREEN was selected for most vegetation.

Here's an even trickier challenge if the "mostly green" theory is true. There are tree species in Australia that are not in Europe and other species in Europe that don't grow in Egypt. Of course, there are species in Egypt that don't grow in California and unique species in many different regions of the earth. These species are unique and exclusive of each other. They are not related. So, my question is—"How is it that most vegetation on the entire planet selected GREEN without 'consulting' each other?"

If it is just random luck that nearly every single vegetation species selected GREEN, that's an awful lot of luck floating around.

We all know it wasn't intelligence that selected GREEN for the entire plant kingdom from the beginning—since that's what we have been taught to believe. It wasn't design. It was plain luck and coincidence. You think?

Nothing As Lovely As A Tree

Trees are commonplace. Sadly, it is not so common for people to appreciate the wonder of trees. They are simply fantastic examples of a highly superior invention in addition to their beauty.

The trees in your yard have these incredible features. First, the roots are each fitted with a protective cap. Good idea, since they are pushing soil. Each cap is lubricated with oil. Sounds like some of us guys who like to put WD-40 on everything but I'm sure it helps.

Not only do the roots hold the tree up making it sturdy, they also function in the feeding of the tree. Behind the caps are root hairs that absorb both water and minerals, which travel up little channels (good thinking) in the wood all the way up to the leaves.

Now could you make one of these? Nobody—no scientist, inventor, university— nobody can make a tree.

How does the water travel from the roots all the way up the tree right out to the leaves? How would you design it? Well, the system already in place works on trees even hundreds of feet tall. That's a pretty good pump. Root pressure starts it but in the trunk, a second system kicks in. Water molecules hold onto each other. The fancy word is "cohesion," meaning to stick or hold together. They stick together like a long rope from the leaves all the way down to the roots. As leaves release moisture into the air, water is evaporating. The tiny columns of water that stick together move up to fill the void as though the rope was being pulled up. This sap/water moves at about 200 feet per hour.

By the way, that moisture released into the air is recycling water that will return again as rain. Not a bad idea, really.

You probably remember photosynthesis from school. The green leaves were way ahead of any solar cells invented by men. They use the energy from the sun plus the carbon dioxide that is already in the air and the water from the roots. With this recipe the leaves make sugar, and in the process what is left to throw away is oxygen. This so-called accidental system created by accident billions of years ago (I scoff) involves seventy (70) separate chemical reactions. Photosynthesis occurs inside tiny cell bodies called "chloroplasts." Now talk about miniaturization, this makes our silicon chips look primitive. Not only do the chloroplasts continually execute this sophisticated process but they also have the ability to grow and reproduce. By the way, you could fit about 400,000 chloroplasts onto the period at the end of any sentence in this article.

Trees are the perfect factories. They are extremely proficient, quiet, non-polluting and even better, contributing to the environment. What most of the world really loves about trees is their beauty. They are tall, strong masters, providing homes and food for wildlife; reproducing so well that they create their own communities of forests and jungles all over the world. They are so widespread in their existence they are a primary habitat for living things. They literally feed the world.

A lucky series of accidents creating such magnificent wisdom is what we are taught.

Look at your tree again. Engineering without an engineer, ingenious ideas without a genius, inventions without an inventor, intelligence without intelligence?

CONNECT THE DOTS

A person who can wire a house has a bigger intellectual challenge than a person who can change a light bulb. A cook who can prepare an eight-course meal for a wedding reception is doing far more than one who fries two eggs.

The more complicated a design, the more brains it takes to put it together. I can make a shoebox but not a piano.

Consider any one oak tree and connect the dots. Here is a tree that cannot live on its own. Even if it sits all alone in a vast field, it is very connected. First, it couldn't grow in a bed of plastic shredding or a heap of metal junk. It needs the dirt. It finds nutrition there and with the same root system, it holds itself steady. Oak trees can penetrate as deeply as one-hundred feet to find water. It needs the soil nutrients and the water too. For the leaves to convert to food, it needs the sun for a very complex yet brilliantly simple process called "photosynthesis." All species need to reproduce or they cease to exist. The seeds, in this case they are acorns, need to be spread. You can't just grow a forest immediately below the branches of one tree. Gravity on a hill helps spread acorns but critters that take the acorns somewhere farther away are also helping make an oak forest. Squirrels and birds do for the oak some things it cannot do for itself.

So far, the trees' survival is dependent on soil, water, sun, birds and/or squirrels. The mighty oak really does need help. Actually, most oaks have leaves that change colors annually. Not in March or July but always in the autumn. In the oak is a clock triggered by the seasons, but what triggers those seasons? It is the orbit of earth. The tilt of the planet as it takes 365 ¼ days to revolve around the sun is what creates summer, autumn, winter and spring to be the same time each year.

It is this seasonal clock that determines, for the oak and many other occurrences of nature, the seasons for specific activities. Each spring, little buds appear on the winter barren oaks and baby leaves mature into green foliage through the remainder and through the hot summer until the leaves turn color. Then, they give up and drop to the ground from which the tree originally emerged. Here the leaves begin enriching the soil with more nutrients which will ultimately feed the new, budding leaves of spring.

This whole cycle is in sync with the seasons. So we must add our orbiting planet to the list of utilized necessities for your oak tree.

Now I ask you, how hard would it be for you to create the same list of necessary assistance for the oak? I suppose it would be challenging enough to invent nutritious dirt, flying birds, reproducing squirrels and a well-timed orbit of something as large as our earth, but then you need to arrange all of them into coordinated interactive systems to fulfill the needs of your oak tree.

Sound like intelligence and power?

In The Kitchen
Alibrando's Law #10
Expert Opinion

Un-provable Notion: If you disagree with an expert you must be wrong.

Sensible Fact: An expert opinion is still an opinion.

Technical Wording: *An expert opinion is still an opinion, not fact.*

Here's a good equation to remember:

$$\text{Opinion} = \text{Opinion}$$
$$\text{Opinion} \neq \text{Fact}$$

Explaining the Law
This is actually important to remember for all of our life in every category.

Experts are people with their own ideas and opinions. Although an expert opinion carries much more weight than a non-expert opinion, it is still an opinion.

An expert, according to one dictionary, is "a person who has special knowledge or skill in a particular field."

The same dictionary defines "opinion" like this: "… judgment or belief resting on grounds insufficient to produce certainty."

Put it together and what do you have? A smart person who can't really be sure. That's what an expert opinion is. So don't hesitate to question any expert opinion.

An opinion may be correct, but it could be incorrect. An opinion is an opinion is an opinion. An opinion, by definition is simply not a fact.

LAW #10
An expert opinion is still an opinion, not fact.

RELATED ARTICLES:
Whodunnit?

PINE CONES
There are many pine trees in the California foothills, especially the more you climb in altitude. The higher you go, the denser the pine trees become and the more interesting pine cones become.

Many of you don't realize there are male and female pinecones.

Even stranger, is that there are male and female pinecones on the same trees.

Most locals have probably seen the yellowish powder on pinecones. That is the pollen. The pollen comes from the male cones.

The pines are dependent on the wind to carry the yellow pollen from the male pinecones to the female pinecones.

That yellow powder (pollen) has to mature before being blown around to female cones.

In the pine tree, that may be as long as three years. That is why you see cones that are all locked up shut and other pine cones that are open like a blossomed flower. The locked up cones are holding the pollen until it matures. When mature, and not before, it will begin to open, allowing the wind to blow its pollen to a female cone. The cone somehow has either a clock or a triggering mechanism to delay its opening.

Unlike the white talcum powder we put on a baby's bottom, this yellow powder, when properly adhered to a female cone, has the ability to draw nourishment from the soil and water, know up from down and respectively sprout one way and dig in roots the other way. The pollen has within itself the blueprint to manufacture a sapling that grows needle-shaped or scale-like "leaves" that stay green all year. The tree grows straight and tall and its entire shape is usually like an upside down cone. It is functional, has protective bark and a whole system of up and down veins for sharing nutrition and growth. This makes the yellow powder an actual blueprint; sophisticated to say the least.

In addition to all this "talent" built into the fine, powdery substance that utilizes its natural environment to become such a huge, organized mass of tree, it also makes more male and female cones so we can have forests throughout the earth.

Not all cones are pinecones. The term "coniferous trees" just means trees that reproduce using cones. That includes our big redwood trees, sequoias, cedar trees, all fir trees, and all pine trees.

There are about five-hundred & fifty types of conifers (and I bet you can't recognize even ten different kinds—me either).

Now I pose the question; does this seem smart to you?

The Meaning Of Leaf

Anyone anywhere need only pick a leaf from any tree or bush in his or her own yard, take it to any well-financed laboratory and write them a check for $1,000,000,000 (one billion dollars), with the express understanding that they cannot cash it until they have created, NOT CLONED, a leaf equally alive and functional. Don't worry. Your check won't bounce; they will never be able to do it because:

1. They have to create tiny plumbing for the leaf veins.
2. They must design and manufacture a system to move the sap through the veins.
3. They must design and manufacture a photosynthesis mechanism that goes beyond solar power, because it must CONVERT carbon dioxide, water and elements into food for itself using the sun.
4. They have to design and manufacture a way for the leaf to metabolize the food. It must be able to use the food as fuel and function using that food/fuel to do everything it does.
5. They will have to design and manufacture an exhaust system for the leaf to rid itself of unwanted material. To copy the real leaf, the wasted exhaust must be oxygen.
6. They must design and manufacture a process that stimulates a branch to initiate creating a bud emerging from just below its surface and the bud must emerge in a forward angle.
7. It will have to have a designed and manufactured system enabling the leaf to literally grow while proportionately expanding its own network of veins and built-in functioning systems.

8. The growth pattern must match the specific, unique design of the species being copied.

9. The leaf must STOP growing at the uniform size considered the normal size.

10. They must design and manufacture a light-sensing system that mechanically turns the darker, light-absorbing side of the leaf toward the light after sensing its light source.

11. They will have to make the underside of the leaf tender and porous in order to absorb available moisture from the morning dew.

12. They must design and manufacture a timing system that will coordinate with other leaves so that in the autumn (or whatever is normal for that species, the leaf stops functioning and "dies" by changing colors and dropping off the tree.

13. To be environmentally safe, after "dying" the leaf must become a stiff brown material that decomposes, enriching soil that feeds the same tree.

14. All of the designed and manufactured systems must be miniaturized to microscopic proportions and work silently without batteries, electricity, combustible fuel or nuclear power. They should interact without need for maintenance.

15. To really be identical the tree should have the ability to repeat all these functions not just once or twice, but flawlessly throughout its lifetime as it continues growing larger and larger. But since the deal is just for the leaf, forget #15.

We aren't asking too much are we? After all, these kinds of things could simply be designed and manufactured by mistake. At least, that's one theory.

Talking Trees

Movies are much scarier now, but as a kid those talking trees in the Wizard of Oz scared me. Not as scary, is the discovery of communication between trees. It is not entirely new. Even in encyclopedias published in the late 70's research was being published regarding this topic.

The first surprise to me is that trees can emit various chemicals. For years, scientists assumed it was different kinds of waste, however, the more we study nature, the more intelligence we discover about it. Chemicals affect the flavor of the tree or leaves.

In the spring of 1979, scientist Davey Rhoades was studying what happens to willow trees when tent caterpillars attack. He had two groups of trees. One group he intentionally infested with the caterpillars. The other nearby group of willows he left alone. The attacked trees had produced a nasty-tasting chemical that discouraged the growth of the caterpillars.

Now before I go any further, I find this fascinating. I always imagined trees as passive things, just sitting there soaking up the sun and growing. A tree or plant cannot run from its enemies but is equipped with an amazing array of chemical defenses. Trees combat hundreds of enemies, year in and year out. A hundred different species of insects and worms, bacteria, fungi, all threatening the life of the tree, must be defeated for the tree to survive.

Back to the experiment; what Rhoades discovered was that the un-attacked trees had produced this same nasty-tasting chemical WITHOUT being attacked. Why? He checked to make sure their roots were not connected. They were not. He disclosed his conclusions three years later after more research. Here was his conclusion: The attacked trees emitted a chemical into the air after being attacked. More amazingly, the un-attacked trees responded to that chemical and flooded their leaves with the chemical that tasted bad and slowed the growth of their enemies—in defense BEFORE they were attacked. Communication between trees, WOW!

Many other names have been added to the list of researchers studying the process of chemical communication between trees. We now know that plants and trees carry and release not only thousands of chemical compounds, but do it in an ever changing manner in response to immediate conditions. Most of these functions are not even cataloged.

Some of the more common chemical weapons are:
1. Tannins, which gives the insect a bad case of indigestion.
2. Alkaloids, which wreak havoc with the insect's nervous system.
3. Dummy amino acids that produce defective proteins inside the insect. Pretty slick, chemical warfare, huh?

Incredibly, the trees can synthesize them on the spot, in hours or days.

Communication between trees may also help coordinate simultaneous flowering for fast cross-pollination. Why would trees benefit from flowering at the same time? There are a couple reasons. One, the flowers attract insects that can cross pollinate. If they are all flowering at the same time the insects will be attracted in bigger numbers and available to pollinate all the flowers while they are there instead of making a separate trip for one or two trees. Secondly, when the fruit grows at the same time, the entire generation of fresh fruit is shorter. Otherwise, if one tree is beginning to have rotten fruit and attracting flies and maggots, the maggots can prematurely destroy the other trees that are just beginning to bear fruit before they rot. By having simultaneous flowering and maturity, maggots don't have as much time to reproduce and devastate the crop.

"Okay everybody, on three—one-two-three—BLOOM!"

There is certainly more I could tell you but I want you to ponder the complexity and organization of such fine design in the trees all around us. The greatest minds of science are still scratching their heads trying to figure out this communication that is so beneficial and impressive. Do you really think this communication between trees could be a random mistake that was never designed? Or do you think it is not a mistake and that these designs are intentional?

IN THE KITCHEN
Alibrando's Ripple 1 of Law #10
Expert Fallibility

If you throw a pebble in still water, it makes a series of circles moving ever outward, commonly called "ripples." Understanding something new for the 1st time can have the same effect. One new idea touches other things by sheer logic. If this is true then that must be true. If that is true then this also must be true, etc.

> *Law #10 stated: An expert opinion is still an opinion.*
> *This is the 1st ripple of that same idea.*

UN-PROVABLE NOTION: Once a person has an impressive enough resume, he can no longer make mistakes related to his field of expertise.

SENSIBLE FACT: No one is always right.

TECHNICAL WORDING: *There is no college degree, profession or training that elevates a person to infallibility.*

Here's a little something to keep in mind.

Certificate ≠ Perfection
A certificate DOES NOT REMOVE
the ability to make mistakes.

EXPLAINING THE LAW

Anyone can be wrong. Anyone can make a mistake. Anyone can operate on a wrong assumption. Those who declare themselves excused from having to prove their ideas should be listened too much more cautiously. In all science, provable facts are *always* necessary. Proof is what makes it scientific.

It should be noted that a person of high standing is in a position to mislead far more people than a person of less influence or credibility. If their information is incorrect more folks are misdirected than somebody talking at the dinner table.

In my way of thinking, an influential expert should be held to a higher standard of proof simply because his or her influence is greater.

RIPPLE 1 OF LAW #10

There is no college degree, profession or training that elevates a person to infallibility.

CHLOROPLASTS—LITTLE GREEN MIRACLES

When you think of chaos, do you think of patterns? When you think of chaos, do you think of order? Me either. When you think of random accidents, do you expect improvement? Me either.

Imagine for a moment, an abandoned castle in a jungle built 5,000 years ago. Animals run through it, ransacking what they can. Insects make homes there; the wind brings dirt and pollen. The rain and sun beat on it for many centuries. After all that time and chance, do you expect it to be a more beautiful castle? Well, that is the overall theory of evolution—time and chance makes for greater order.

Miniaturization is a quest that continues even now in all circuitry and other components. Computers that once filled buildings were reduced to one room. Eventually they were reduced to just one wall-size but could do even more than their predecessors could. Now laptop computers can do immeasurably more than the building-size granddaddy computer ever dreamed and nano-technology is happening now.

I have had watch-size calculators on my wrist. The computer chip, itself, is a fascinating study of miniaturization of tiny circuitry.

Now let's look at one of nature's miniature wonders, the chloroplast. The chloroplast is what makes your grass, leaves and pine needles green. It's the green you see in nearly all vegetation. Chloroplast is not just a color. It is considerably more sophisticated than a micro-chip. It is more like a micro-manufacturing plant.

A manufacturing plant normally takes certain raw materials and converts them into products to sell. For instance, I worked at a paneling factory in New Jersey. The "raw" materials delivered to the plant were plywood sheets, paints and chemicals. We had the machinery, manpower, technology and know-how to create lovely paneling for homes.

A single microscopic chloroplast is like a manufacturing plant. Let's consider the chloroplasts in tree leaves. It takes only sunlight and water as raw material. The water is delivered through the tree's veins. Water travels from the roots through the trunk through the branches and then to the leaves. Just to be efficient, the undersides of leaves are not shiny but more porous so it can retain more moisture from the morning dew and raindrops that roll to the underside before falling to the ground.

The GREEN is used to absorb sunlight. This is an important job for the leaf. The machinery, manpower, and know-how are all within the chloroplast to create food (glucose) for the whole community within the tree (roots, trunk, branches and leaves).

This food manufacturing process we call "photosynthesis." This is no slap-happy, whoops, whadya know it works, kinda thing. It is a highly organized, complex and finely tuned engine with highly rated efficiency.

EFFICIENCY is measured as a ratio of output to input power expressed as a percentage. With the paneling factory, our wastes (or by-products) were chemical odors, lots of defective panels, left-over chemicals, broken machine parts and left-over packaging and shipping materials.

The chloroplast has much less waste. It has only one waste product, that waste product is oxygen. Oxygen, as you know, is critical to all biological life forms on earth. Gee, that's kind of useful. This was invented before "recycling" was popular.

Our paneling factory was dependent on the utility company for electricity, wood mills to give us our "raw" already fabricated plywood, cardboard manufacturing plants for packaging, all of which had their own additional waste products. We also depended on chemical companies for stains, coatings, and cleaning machinery—and they have plenty of harmful waste. We had to depend on other companies to supply our machines, parts, and of course, we needed the trucking companies to ship us materials and to deliver our finished products. All of these have their own costs and wastes.

The chloroplast is part of a living cell and has everything it needs to start and finish the complete job except for its need for sunshine and water, that's it. The chloroplasts not only have the ability, but the "brains" to know how to derive the water and mix it with sunlight in correct proportions and then process these elements. Do you think you could explain exactly how this is done since it is just a dumb plant? Actually, it is far less than a plant and is less than a complete cell. It is merely a part of the plant cell. The process of photosynthesis which I am describing is a complex seventy-stage exercise, ultimately manufacturing its final product. I said *seventy stages*! This is much more complicated than our paneling factory. This is much more sophisticated than our paneling factory. This is far more efficient than our paneling factory and far more impressive. Can you imagine how long my article would be if I described individually all seventy steps? I don't even want to do all that research let alone write about it.

The finished product (nutrition) is then "delivered" to the "community" (the rest of the tree). Life is sustained in the tree and it continues to grow for another season. When the green leaves die in the autumn they drop below the branches but above the roots; providing more nutrients to be fed to the tree with the help of those roots. This is additional recycling—making "waste" a useful and valuable by-product. So now it is not waste.

Overall, it's not too shabby an operation. There is more information on the internet revealing how vast and still impossible it is to fully understand the complex, yet efficient workings of chloroplast; the green within the cells that works so very well.

PLANTS DON'T LOOK SMART TO ME

It has always fascinated me how attracted we are to foods that are bad for us. Candy, cake, coffee, greasy fries and burgers, salty chips, sweet soda and almost anything else that will cause cancer, hardened arteries, or create fat.

I try to read labels and avoid some things but where are my instincts that should know what my body needs?

Plants and trees have this amazing ability to turn toward the sun. That may not seem like a big deal to you, but to me they just never seemed smart enough to know how, or more specifically, that they should know they needed to turn toward the light and actually *do* it.

There's more. Check this out. You know how you misplace your pen all the time?

"Hey, where did I put my pen? It was right here a minute ago. Who took it?"

It seems experiments have proven that plants have a real good memory when it comes to where they saw the light last. To me, they just don't look that smart.

In one experiment, they flash a light for a fraction of a second. Over the next couple of days, with no more light, the plant slowly grows and turns toward that light, or at least where it was last "seen."

Energy companies, private businesses, and naturally we taxpayers, spend millions of dollars on light tracking systems for solar power and space satellites.

It isn't easy to engineer sensors that understand, "Oh hey, the light is over there guys."

On space satellites, batteries run the motors that direct the panels to turn them toward where the sensors say the light is. It is a computerized tracking system; software that knows where the light should be on a certain date if the satellite is in a certain location. This is all very high tech and expensive. The rechargeable battery-operated motors turn the solar panels toward the sun with its gears and rods so the angle is maximized.

Do you have a flower in the window? It does the same thing and it didn't cost you millions. It detects the light with superior software. It translates the information and it has "muscles" or "motors" to turn, usually at a ninety-degree angle toward the light.

Some ivy plants even dodge each other's leaf shade so each leaf can get the maximum amount of light. Imagine trying to develop additional "software" that triggers a "dodging" response. It would also have to motorize and prolong stems to reach beyond the shade of other ivy leaves. Hundreds of leaves all programmed to arrange themselves in a systemized pattern so they are right next to each but with minimum or zero overlap.

I am so impressed because frankly, those plants and trees just don't look that smart.

INSECTS

A Fairy Tale Of Sorts

A Wife That Is Thousands Of Times Heavier Than Her Husband

Although sometimes called "white ants" termites are not ants at all but more related to roaches. They are on every continent except Antarctica. More than 2,000 species have already been categorized. The African termites build huge above-ground mounds. Like ants, they live in colonies with everyone having very specific and life-long tasks; workers, soldiers, gardeners, builders and of course the king and queen. The queen is the big shot. Life pretty much rotates around the queen but she does her part too. She puts out about 30,000 eggs every day. Boy, keep her away from my house. She may live a surprisingly long life for an insect. In her case, 20 years. If you want to multiply 30,000 eggs a day times 365 days a year times 20 years, go ahead. She is also much larger than her king and is literally thousands of times heavier. I read it takes the king fifteen seconds just to walk from one end of his wife to the other. He must be slow because she is only about 4 inches long and about the width of a man's thumb. I must admit 4 inches is a huge termite.

The soldiers are interestingly all female. They don't cook either. As a matter of fact, they can't even feed themselves because of their extra large heads that are shaped for fighting and somewhat armored. So worker termites feed the soldiers.

The workers are both male and female. They feed the soldiers, the babies, the king and the queen. Other worker termites do either building or gardening. That's another article.

They all live in total darkness and do not have eyes. Several nights a year, however, something magical happens. Some of the young termites are somehow selected to become princes and princesses. The new royalty are now granted what none of the others have—eyes to see. There is more magic. They miraculously sprout wings and behold, they can fly. The newly selected royalty fly out from their darkness in swarms. With their new eyes they are seeing everything. From within the swarm, each prince finds a princess. They will separate from the swarm, the two of them. Together they select a location that will become their own community that they will rule as king and queen. They land. They shed their wings. They dig down and build a small underground room and seal themselves inside. Once again in the dark, they mate. They will build their kingdom from their offspring. They never need to see again and lose their eyesight. Like all queens and kings, they will never leave their room. Workers will tend to all their needs. The princess, now a queen, begins laying eggs creating a completely new community.

What scientists cannot figure out is how identical eggs hatch into identical nymphs but then become different kinds of termites. Even more mysterious is that if there is a shortage of soldiers a higher ratio of nymphs become soldiers, if they need builders, more become builders. What I don't get is why the queen becomes huge and the king stays a shrimp.

The society, the instincts fulfilling their function, the workers, the soldiers, the builders, the princes and princesses, the magical moment of seeing and flying, all adds up to a highly structured community with diverse yet predictable abilities. It is a species that has successfully survived doing exactly what it is doing today; a species less intelligent than man yet accomplishing feats in a manner beyond the comprehension of man. It's another testimony of intelligent design, intelligence greater than our own.

GRASSHOPPER

Crickets, grasshoppers and katydids! Have you ever seen more than 10,000 all at the same time? Well, it is possible that you could look at more than 10,000 of these critters and not have two of them be the same species! Scientists have discovered more than 10,000 different species: crickets—1,000, grasshoppers—5,000 and katydids—4,000. There are certainly plenty more yet to be discovered.

There are researchers out there who have studied one or two species for years. It is overwhelming how many species there are. We look at just about any insect and call it a "bug." Just get it out of the house or off my arm, right? But when researchers take the time to document their findings, we learn that each species has its own way of reproducing, growing, getting its food, flying, "singing" and other behavioral traits. Of these 10,000 species, naturally, they only mate within their species.

Not one single species can science recreate. The technology is out of reach. Maybe they can take DNA and move stuff around, but they can't *make* that DNA. They might clone, but they can't *make* the stuff they clone from.

For example, some grasshoppers can jump 100 times their length. Okay, that's like a 5-foot tall kid jumping 500 feet! There are no human legs or machine that can do that on earth. A standing jump of 500 feet is easily clearing a forty-story building. I don't know of any machine that can leap over a one story house, let alone a two, three, five, ten or twenty story building.

We already have the prototype—a grasshopper—we have the dimensions, the materials. Even with it right there for us to examine, with all our technology and computers, we still can't devise anything near it. The technology we examine is too far out of reach.

There are about 10 species of swarming locusts. Surprisingly, the same swarming species will usually go for years living peacefully and unnoticed. Who rallies and leads these guys? Nobody really knows. The other 4,990 grasshopper species are usually alone except to mate.

Can such technologically advanced order come by chaos and accident? If the greatest brains can't figure it out, why say it took no brains to design it?

Most grasshoppers can fly too. Grasshoppers have been sighted by radar taking off in enormous numbers as night falls and flying with the wind as high as 3,000 feet and traveling 200–300 miles in a few days.

One column of flying locusts, short-horned grasshoppers, seen over the Red Sea was estimated to be 2,000 miles long! That would be a solid stretch of locusts from California to Ohio! I have read that the roar of huge locust swarms' wings is deafening as they approach like a huge, black storm.

How powerful they become in such large numbers. Who leads them? Why are they united? What is the purpose? Are these not amazing facts and wonders for science to ponder and leave so many questions unanswered?

INSECTS—MICRO MACHINES
Often we bypass the wonder of massive things and pay more attention to the simple. For example, if I said there were 46,751,654,000,000 stars you would probably believe me. But if I paint a bench and post a "WET PAINT" sign, you want to see if it's really true so you touch the paint. (By the way, I made up that star number.)

Insects are vast and numerous. Like the stars, they are too vast to comprehend, but analyzed individually, they are fascinating. Can you imagine being able to name every bug you ever swatted? People would think you were a genius.

How do they work? How do they keep on surviving despite superior man's effort to eliminate them?

One encyclopedia lists 25,000 species of bugs. "Bugs" are actually a sub-category of insects. But there are more than 750,000 species of insects. It is believed there are four times that number yet to be discovered and categorized (three million). Can you name 10 bugs? Me either. Nope, spiders are not insects.

Insects are everywhere except the two polar caps. Insects are not just creepy, crawly things. They have been spotted as high as 10,000 feet.

Would people think you were smart if you told them that ALL adult insects have their bodies divided into head, thorax, and abdomen (head, middle, and end)? The middle part is what has the six legs on the insect where the wings are also attached.

Here are more characteristics of ALL insects. Their digestive system seems like a simple tube but is actually ten parts starting at the mouth and ending up, well you know. They manufacture digestive juices too. All insect jaws work at right angles biting *inward* from side to side.

Bet you don't think of an insect as having a heart. They do. Their heart is a series of pumping chambers with an upper tube. They move their colorless blood by squeezing. They even have a measurable pulse that ranges from as high as 140 times a minute for active insects to a slowed pulse rate of about 1 per hour for chilled insects.

They breathe by taking in air through a series of holes.

Now don't forget, what I am telling you even applies to those tiny gnats we can hardly see. I have a little mini-microscope that enlarges only ten times with a light. It is my son's. Every time I swat some little tiny bug that goes to my computer screen or arm, I try not to squash it too much. I then look at it through that magnifier/microscope. Wow! They all look so high tech under that little magnifier. So alien and science-fiction looking, not the speck I thought I was swatting at all.

Now what I am telling you below, is what I read not saw.

Insects have a nervous system that looks like a ladder on their lower inner surface.

Not much of a brain, more like a glob of nerve cells in the head. Maybe that's why a locust can go on living for two hours after having his head cut off (doesn't take much brain to be a locust, I guess). But it sure takes brains to design a locust, or any insect.

Their three-layered skin is important because of its flexibility, hardness, and waterproof quality.

Reproduction? Boy, can they reproduce. Some termites lay 2,000–3,000 eggs a day. Some of those egg-laying mama termites live fifteen to twenty years cranking out eggs almost every day.

Interestingly, 85% of insect species develop by a process of complete METAMORPHOSIS, for which the butterfly is famous. Caterpillars and butterflies are not two species but one, like maggots and flies. Complete metamorphosis means the creature changes not only in shape but also internally. This isn't a makeover. Their internal organs even change.

An article ten times the length of this could be written about nearly any aspect of any specific insect because they are intricate, complicated machines beyond the full comprehension of science. Even bugs prove how inferior our science is in designing and miniaturizing.

Oooo, A Bug!

We have invented ways of hiding our vast ignorance of the multitude of species with words that seem to show we have identified a creature; "Oooo, a bug." A bug? "Bug" is a species?

"Well, there are so many insects, 'bug' covers most of them," you may say.

Amazingly, there are experts out there who study certain "bugs" so thoroughly that they can tell us the areas of the world in which they live, what they eat, how they mate and reproduce, their lifespan, their natural enemies, how they fight or hide, approximately how many babies they have per year, how they travel and where they might go. Then they may tell you about some of the sub-species in other areas and the differences in behavior. This may all be about one "bug."

When I actually looked up the word "bug" in an encyclopedia it said "see Hemiptera." I had never even heard that word. It is pronounced, "hem-ip'-tur-uh." That doesn't even rhyme with any words I know. Many of our words come from Latin but this one comes from Greek. It is two words meaning "half" and "wings." Hemi is half.

These seemingly endless details and huge numbers are the kind of stuff that starts to shut our brain down. Things so vast are too hard to take in. On top of that, we start introducing Greek and Latin names of species categories then we really close down our brain and go watch some TV show that requires absolutely no thinking, and I'm sure it must shrink our brain.

What we are missing is how interesting some of these "bugs" really are. I admit, if they fly around my head I swat at them and wish they were dead. But in addition to providing tons of food for birds, there really is some interesting stuff here.

Somebody went to the trouble to categorize about 25,000 species of Hemiptera (bugs). What a job, huh? They all have certain characteristics, like those that can pierce and suck. Yuck! No wonder we go "Oooo, a bug" just before we squash it. Of these 25,000 species most have not one, but two pairs of wings. Most have antennas instead of cable (that's a joke). Seriously, somebody has been counting the segments on these 25,000 species and they say that they must have either four or five segments on the antennas. If you don't see any antennas, it is because some are hidden.

Now if there were really such a thing as evolution you would think you would at least have a few squirrels with antennas or some birds that had two sets of wings.

Fortunately for us all, "bugs" don't get bigger than four inches, according to the article. That's big enough for me because it would be pretty gross trying to squash a foot-long bug, let alone swat at it.

Whoever divided up the 25,000 species bug world wanted to simplify things a little so he (I figure it had to be a guy, we are talking about bugs, here) made three easy categories; land, water, and in-between (shores). There are even bugs in the ocean.

The thing is how all this bug stuff works so incredibly well. I'm inspired.

SPECIFIC CREATURES

BATS

The smallest bat in the world is the bumblebee bat. It weighs less than a penny. The largest is the giant flying fox bat of Indonesia having a wingspan of nearly six feet. Vampire bats are in Central America only—no place else in the wild. The entire rest of the world, including Central America, have bats to thank for being the most important natural enemies of night-flying insects, especially mosquitoes.

The most common bat here in California and in the world, is the little brown bat. The little brown bat eats near 600 insects an hour, more than a whole group of us can swat. That is a whole lot more efficient than those *"electrocute the mosquitoes"* contraptions that bring us such sadistic pleasure each time we hear that "zap." Oh yeah, another one bites the dust.

I don't know how many hours a day a bat feeds but let's just say three hours. Because of one brown bat, 1,800 insects are removed from bugging us every day. If there were ten brown bats in the neighborhood, that neighborhood would have 18,000 less bugs every single day. In a week 126,000 bugs would be removed by only ten of our brown bat friends. That is over a quarter million less insects in just two weeks. Wow! Give me bats for my birthday.

A colony of one hundred fifty brown bats can protect a local farmer from 18 million or more rootworms each summer.

Doesn't it sound like these bats are doing us a big favor? Shouldn't we be recruiting these guys? By the way, they don't have rabies any more than cats or dogs would. They need a public relations agent.

More than 50% of American bat species are in severe decline or already listed as endangered. Even though bats can live up to thirty years, they don't reproduce in quantity or great frequency. A mother bat has only one "pup" a year.

Pesticides kill off the bats' food supply. Unfortunately, although pesticides are used for killing insects, they can also poison the bats. This creates a vicious cycle. Once the bat population is significantly lowered, the insect population climbs out of control creating a greater need for artificial (chemical) control, which again decreases the bat population . . .

One funny thing, all these bat scientists, according to my reading, don't really know where most male bats go in the summer! In hide and seek, the bats are winning.

Science often copycats ideas from nature. Why not? Nature's design is of superior design and intelligence. Radar came after the discovery of the bat's "echo-location." By hearing how the sound waves (pulse beeps) bounce back to him, the bat can quickly locate his bug. "Echo-Location"; that's how we got the idea to invent radar.

But wait, there's more. Where did we get the stealth idea? You know the multi-billion dollar project of making a plane that is invisible to radar. Was it man's genius?

It's funny how creatures are given special abilities to not only catch their food, but sometimes to simply avoid being eaten. Bats also eat moths. Some simple moths have a fascinating special ability. They can send pulse beeps back to the bat confusing the bat's echo-location. The beeps the moth sends to the bat makes the bat think he has found another bat. Since bats don't eat bats, the moth is safe.

This is how the stealth works. It doesn't actually hide from radar. It sends back "beeps" that makes probing radar believe it is not there. Those beeps can also make radar think it is smaller than it actually is, or going a different speed than it really is.

So, who is the brain behind the stealth moth?

THOSE AMAZING SALMON

How do birds *not* get lost? People say they go south for the winter but most kids, and quite a few adults, don't even know which way south is.

Maybe birds can steer as they look down, but how do fish navigate under water, especially Salmon who travel thousands of miles?

Crossover from country to rock music isn't half as interesting as Salmon that crossover from fresh water to salt water and back.

Salmon travel without the help of maps, an auto club or satellite.

Millions of dollars of research has gone into trying to figure this out.

The Atlantic salmon build little gravel nests in freshwater and then bury their hatched eggs in freshwater streams. The female lays as many as 20,000 eggs in October or November.

The young migrate to salt water from fresh water after they reach maturity. They float downstream into a bigger creek, which merges with a larger body of water, until they make their way to a river heading out to sea.

It is in the ocean where they grow up and stay for 4–5 years. Grown, mature salmon head back for home. Each generation returns to spawn in exactly the same breeding places as the generation before it, in late spring or early summer.

How do they know it's time? I don't know.

How do they know which way to go, especially from the middle of the ocean, which is much larger than any continent on earth to our vast coastline? I don't know that either.

The Atlantic salmon migrates back to cold, fresh water, swimming upstream at an average rate of up to 4 miles per day. It's all upstream. Salmon can jump as much as 12 feet out of water.

Scientists have tagged salmon and found them thousands of miles from home. They even put them in rivers where they had never been before.

Do you know what happened? They went back out the river, back to the ocean, back to the right river and up the tributaries and streams until they got right back to their true birthplace.

Can you do that? Me either. Have the scientists figured out how the fish do it?

They have a good theory with evidence that salmon use the sun and compensate for the bend in the water, calculating their origin from anywhere on earth. The whole thing is very sophisticated. I tried several times to understand it and I decided maybe salmon can't read and write but they sure can travel with more certainty than I can.

If you could understand just the formula salmon use, you would never, ever get lost on any continent or ocean for the rest of your life. People would think you were a real brain.

Does that mean salmon are more intelligent than most humans are? Of course not, but whatever—whoever put that insight into the salmon is definitely smarter than any human is, since humans can't figure it out or duplicate it.

WOLF TREATY

Politicians are commended if they can get warring nations to agree on a treaty. True diplomats are rare and valuable.

The primary cause of death among wolves is being killed by wolves from other packs—sounds unfriendly.

What can we do to keep them peacefully apart? Not fences throughout the wild, that is unpractical for many reasons. It seems unlikely that we could get animals to cooperate with some "treaty" we could arrange. And if this impossible feat were possible and we can make it work with one generation, what about future generations?

Let's consider the possibility that we could figure out some way to implant a computer chip into every living wolf, utilizing our idea of a treaty and the wolf's natural abilities.

We cannot make them overly calm because taking away their edge to survive would ultimately destroy them. We can decide on a certain amount of space they can protect—a turf. Since wolves roam, these would have to be roaming boundaries. If food is plentiful, the space can be smaller, if food is scarce, by necessity the space would have to be larger. These are many variables and organizing this would require highly sophisticated programming. Our goal is to keep competing wolf packs from running into each other accidentally, which almost always leads to bloodshed and usually death.

Do you see how difficult this problem is for technology? We shall set up a network system of communication so one pack is alerted when another pack is in the vicinity. Wolves can howl, so how can we invent a chip that successfully communicates these ideas and variables while interacting with the wolf brain? We don't really have the resources to track down all the wolves in the wild and implant the chips. But before we even begin to approach that problem, I know we do not have the expertise to design such a computer chip. Anyway, even if we did, before we were done implanting all the wild wolves from this generation, the next generation having no computer chips would be here and all would be needing implantation.

Just this one undertaking poses impossible and monumental intelligence, planning and high maintenance still leaving future generations as an unsolved problem.

The problem is already solved. The solution is in the DNA of every fertilized wolf egg. We take these things for granted not appreciating the marvel of it all.

Howling is the glue that keeps wolf packs together. Because they cover vast areas to find food, often alone, howling is their "walkie-talkie." Wolves can distinguish between the howls of pack members and strange wolves. The young wolf pups have to learn.

Howling works over large distances. Scientists are still trying to understand the specific signals that seem to be universally recognized by wolves for different purposes.

Unlike walkie-talkies, howling is heard by all within its range. It is also the howling that helps keep rival packs from accidentally running into each other. No one wants an unnecessary confrontation.

Intentional attacks have been observed. This would occur for a number of reasons but no pack would attack a larger pack. That makes sense. Small packs that howl their presence to avoid engaging another pack may actually be advertising their vulnerability. This is why small packs may prefer silence when traveling. Where did they get this discriminating wisdom? Large packs howl much more often. They are the big, bad wolves.

When there is a known rivalry building between packs that have not met visibly, small packs employ a clever bluffing strategy. With coordinated effort, just four wolves can create a very difficult chorus as far as estimating the size of the pack. It starts with a single howl followed by a second wolf's howling. The third and fourth enter in, not together but one after the other but joining with more acceleration. At this point, you can count the wolves but then is the fifth howl a fifth wolf or the first wolf joining in at the accelerated pace? As the whole pack is howling, they change pitches more erratically and rapidly in what sounds like chaos. This process takes less than two minutes from the first howl to the silence. Add this to the trees, ridges, rocks, valleys and you have an environment that may bounce the sounds and actually multiply the effect. This can cause four wolves to sound like eight or sixteen. This is called the "Beau Geste Effect."

It's sophisticated stuff to say the least. Guess what? They don't howl at the moon. That is some dumb human idea. Although wolves may be more active in the light of the moon, the howl is far too important in communicating than to just use it talking to the moon.

So now we can take all this incredible wisdom, communication and strategizing and give it to every generation of wolves whether they know each other or not, via DNA. The chip is already implanted and it is mastermind design.

Drilling Isn't Always Boring

So, do you know what "larva" is? I will tell you. It is that newly hatched insect stage, often wormlike, before it gets its wings and changes into its familiar adult shape (metamorphosis).

The mother Ichneumon Wasp drills for several hours bringing up powdery sawdust as her depth reaches as much as three inches. Another tunnel is reached. Who made the other tunnel? This is what she was aiming for. It is a tunnel drilled by another mother from another species who hoped she was safely hiding her young. Her young are tucked away in their larva stage. Usually the victim larva is caterpillar, but it could be spiders, moths or something else. How the mother wasp detected that there was "hidden" larva in this particular branch at this particular spot is impressive and as yet still not understood by science.

The mother wasp then injects her own eggs into her newly drilled tunnel close to the victim larva. After the wasp larva hatch, they will wriggle through the drilled tunnel and attach themselves to the victim larva. The victim larva becomes a package of food for the wasp eggs. Even at the infant larval stage, there is already predator and prey—bad news for the not-so-well hidden victim larva, good news for the young wasps.

The wasp then spins a cocoon and will change form into what we would recognize as a wasp, although much skinnier than the stinging wasps most of us are familiar with.

This makes for fascinating science but consider the impossibility of these wasps surviving without the tools and know-how.

I had to loosen bolts under a sink where there was no room for a wrench. I tried grabbing them with pliers' points. I was accidentally stripping the nuts and wasting hours.

How many billion years will it take for my pliers to evolve into a tool that works under the sink, because I need it? Stranger still, how many billion years until my own human descendents would grow special tools right from their own body to solve this difficult under the sink problem? Sound crazy? Well, many scientists figure backwards exactly like this. They see a well-equipped creature and explain in textbooks that the creature evolved the necessary tools to find and catch prey, to fight or escape predators. How did they survive those millions of years WITHOUT the necessary tools?

Since I really don't have billions of years and neither does the sink, it is lucky for me that somebody smarter than me already invented a tool to grab those hard-to-grab nuts to loosen the bolts. Somebody else chuckling at my struggle told me about the tool and loaned me his. I later bought one for less than ten dollars.

The inventor was smart enough to come up with a design to solve a problem he must have had too. Either he had the business savvy or right connections to get it patented and then marketed for a profit. My friend was smart enough to buy it and kind enough to tell me about it. I was smart enough to accept a superior idea—brains, brains, brains.

I really don't think some helpless mama wasp, a billion years ago, knew she needed to stick her eggs near another larva to eat but lacked the tools and talent to drill into wood. I don't think thousands or millions of generations of mama and baby wasps died but still survived as a species while waiting to grow body parts that could:

1. Smell prey inside of branches.
2. Drill into the wood three inches deep.

Getting a tool does not make you skilled. These wasps, AFTER growing these new body parts, would also have to evolve the know-how to use these new abilities.

And how about prototypes? Yeah. Practice makes perfect. If DNA is going to invent something to help a species survive, who runs quality control? I can't believe DNA decided when the nose and drilling mechanism was perfect and said, "OK, forget the last 937 prototypes. Let's reproduce this perfect one from now on."

And who "programmed" the wasp hatchlings to instinctively wriggle down the tunnel and attach themselves to the victim larva?

In all cases I think, like me, they got outside help with the tools and expertise from someone smarter than themselves.

DUMB WASPS, SMART ORCHIDS

Why do so many women think men have just one thing on their mind? Why do they get together and talk about how shallow men are?

That is why I am concerned about too many women learning about these wasps in Australia.

You see, this is not only bad for the guys, but this is a case where the plant kingdom outsmarts the animal kingdom. Well, outsmarts at least the "insect kingdom."

There are these orchids in Australia. They have a problem. Like all species, they need to reproduce. They need to get their pollen to other orchids, otherwise no more orchids like this in the world.

You may not know this but transferring pollen (powdery stuff that makes so many of us sneeze) is critical to making fruit. That pollen is really like male sperm to a flower. Wind or creature must move it to other flowers.

So, there is the orchid challenge. The orchids have only one month of the year to spread all of their pollen. Now, how can they make sure it is spread to other orchids to reproduce?

How about this—they put on a costume and pretend they are girl wasps? Sounds crazy, huh? Well, the species of wasp selected is perfect. Here's why.

The species is the Ichnumid Wasp. Every year in Australia, all their male wasps hatch an entire month earlier than the female wasps. Now picture all these guy wasps cruising around Australia and there isn't a single female around on the entire continent.

Guess what? Amazingly, during that exact month, the orchid opens up and looks just like... surprise... one of the girl Ichnumid Wasps—at least to these guy wasps.

Yep, the guy wasps jump on the orchids and while having a great time they get all this pollen all over themselves.

Afterwards, they keep on cruising, hair messed up, and no shower. With all that pollen on them, they spot another unattached "female," or so it appears. The wasps jump on still more orchids, bringing all that messy pollen with them from the last orchid. This is the precious pollen from the other orchids needed for cross-pollination.

Everybody's happy. The orchids go on reproducing thanks to the dumb wasps. No environmental group has to raise money for an endangered orchid, and the wasps tell stories of their party days, never realizing it was not a real girl. The real female wasps must not complain because every year the new batch of boy wasps fall for the same orchid trick.

You don't believe me, do you? You think I'm making this up? If you really want to check it out for yourself, I'll tell you the technical names of the orchid too.

The orchid is called Cryptostylis leptochila and is still imitating the Ichnumid Wasp, both in Australia.

Oh, and ladies, this is one of those freaks of nature; guys aren't really that dumb—or shallow. ☺

In The Kitchen

Alibrando's Law #5
Extinction Science

Un-provable Notion: Prehistoric, extinct species are all ancestors of modern creatures.

Sensible Fact: When a creature becomes extinct it is gone, not evolving.

Technical Wording: *The extinction of a species is not a species mutation.*

The symbols in the graph below represent that a species becoming extinct does not equal a species evolving.

Pretend the letters in this list represent the corresponding species:
A. Primitive fish
B. An underwater fish with legs
C. Amphibious fish (can breathe air or water)
D. Fish with skin instead of scales
E. Primitive lizard

The first "A" ends, symbolizing extinction. Then you see "≠" which means "does not equal." The second "A" becomes extinct but at the same moment a new species emerges creating species "B." Then "B" becomes extinct to start "C" another species and so forth until we see "E," representing the species as we know it today. Is this crazy or what?

```
                                        E----------------|
                             D--------|
                  C--------|
          B---------|
A--------|   ≠   A--------|
```

Explaining the Law:

This is like our modern tiger being a descendent of a saber-toothed tiger which is a descendent of who knows what. Ultimately, we are also supposed to consider it scientific that even the saber-toothed tiger is a descendent of some reptile which is a descendent of some fish with legs. Of course, you are also supposed to believe that the fish with legs is a descendent of fish without legs, which are descendents of simpler life-forms, like squirmy globs that are descendents of some one-celled organism. That is what all the science books teach but they make it sound a lot more scientific than I just did. Think it through for yourself. Isn't this what they are saying?

With every skeleton we unearth that is an extinct species, we are generally told it is some ancestor that evolved into other species.

Whenever we study a living species today, we are usually told it is the descendent of some extinct species. Sometimes this is accompanied with illustrations showing similar anatomy of that extinct "ancestor." Just because the anatomy is similar, we are told this is "proof" but there really is no proof.

With 100% of the cases of extinction we have witnessed and documented, we did not observe evolution—ONLY the end of that species.

Example 1: An extinct Dodo bird is not the ancestor of any new species. The Dodo is merely an extinct bird. The fact that it is similar in design to any other species shows comparable design, not relative origin.

Ironically, we have many laws protecting endangered species. No one considers it strange that scientists who believe the evolutionary theory are also zealous to protect these endangered species. Here is a clue rarely observed: It is because they have ZERO confidence in that species' ability to simply evolve.

Their lack of confidence IS SCIENTIFIC because we see no evidence. We have no confidence. Yet, we are still taught that all creatures that live among us are the result of past evolution from extinct ancestors.

Folks, there is no scientific (meaning proof, not theory) basis for the assumption that any extinct species was necessarily an ancestor of any other species.

Therefore, I feel compelled to state *as a law* that can be proved:

LAW #5
    The extinction of a species is not a species mutation.

RELATED ARTICLES:
Seahorse Sense

SEAHORSE SENSE
When I was little, any kid could buy his own seahorses for his aquarium. Where did they all go?

I didn't give it much thought until I recently read an article about seahorses in a used magazine I bought at the public library. Millions of seahorses are captured and ground up in China, Indonesia, and the Philippines for all kinds of remedies. They are now listed by the World Conservation Union as an endangered species and so seahorses are now being bred in captivity.

They are curious creatures, though. They have been observed greeting each other (the mates) every morning with a dance lasting from five minutes to four hours. This dancing includes the couple dancing in synchronization. That means they are doing the same dance moves in unison as though they practiced together. The show doesn't stop there. They also have dramatic color changes in their body during the dance. Just as oddly, after the dance, they normally go their separate ways for the day. They get back together the next day for the dance again. Some seahorses are thought to mate for life.

Guess who gets pregnant? The male—sort of—the female has no sperm, only eggs, but she deposits those eggs inside the male's pouch. Like a kangaroo, the male seahorse has a pouch called a "brood pouch." It is only after the eggs are in the male's pouch that they are fertilized. Once fertilized, the pouch becomes the incubator for ten days to six weeks as the fertilized eggs mature. The difference in time to mature is based on the size of the seahorse species. It gets more bizarre. The male seahorse actually goes into labor—big time, squirming, twisting and writhing in apparent pain. That's what I read, but it didn't explain what exactly is causing that pain.

As for its eating habits, I had no idea. A two-week old seahorse can eat up to 25 times its body weight. That is like your 30-pound child or grandchild eating 750 pounds of food a day. Folks call ya "pig" if you eat a lot, but no way do pigs eat 25 times their body weight on any day. I admit calling a person "seahorse" doesn't have the same ring to it.

How do you program a color light show, synchronized dancing, the female knowing to put eggs in a male pouch that fertilizes her eggs, male "labor" and an appetite that is almost beyond belief and stick all this in a DNA strand so that the species continues on like that for all generations?

I recently read elsewhere that there were far *less* species in the world today than there used to be. Sure, no more dinosaurs, Dodo birds and other animals. This can be easily proven and documented. Scientists have a fascinating and long list of extinct species. But the evolutionary theory generally claims a different idea: One species becomes five species, which create twenty-five more which create another one-hundred and twenty-five and so on, like some grand multi-level marketing species invention program. If that is the true pattern, we should have MORE species today than ever, not less and less species like we know is true.

Now why does it seem like there are so many facts in different arenas that are easily observable yet contradict the basic theory of evolution? Let's put more good ol' fashioned horse sense back into science.

A Feather Is No Light Matter

There are so many wondrous things around us, we hardly notice. It is not unusual to see a feather on the ground as we are walking. Next time, pick it up and observe it carefully. You will see that the feather, if not too ruffled, somehow holds itself together—tightly.

If you have a microscope at home, you can really have fun with this. Look at the feather under the microscope and you will see little hooks holding the "strands" of feather together. They are more like barbs. It works like Velcro or even more like a zipper.

Out of the shaft (thick middle part) of the feather are the strands going outward. Those strands of the feather are called "barbs." There are three kinds of barbs in the typical feather. From largest to smallest they are barbs, barbules and barbicels.

The feather can often be separated and then smoothed back together. The reason they can be smoothed back together is because the barbules and barbicels re-hook like a zipper. Each barb has many barbules. Each barbule has hundreds of barbicels (hooklets). A single pigeon feather has several hundred thousand barbules and millions of barbicels. Sounds organized, huh?

A bird the size of a swan has some 25,000 feathers. Wanna try the barbicel math?

Feathers grow like hair from a follicle but instead of hair, the hollow quill emerges. The quill was used for years as a pen because of its construction. The shaft of the quill has a spongy center with air-filled cells; obviously, a design for lightweight strength.

Often around the neck, head and underbody are "filoplumes." These filoplumes are hair like feathers having a slender shaft with few or no barbs.

All the feathers grow in patterns along most bird's bodies. The feathers are carefully placed so overlapping feathers cover bare patches of skin.

Birds molt (shed) their feathers, one or more times annually. Some birds molt an equal number of feathers on each wing so they can maintain balance during flight. Boy, that's important. Many waterfowl breeds, such as ducks, will molt their flight feathers all at once. The feathers must be critical to enabling birds to fly, because the ducks cannot fly until the feathers are renewed.

There are flight feathers categorized "primary" and "secondary" for the wing. Tail feathers are of a different design, which allow birds to control lift, steering, and braking during flight. Naturally, to have all of this highly engineered flying design would be useless if the instinct to use it properly were not imbedded as well, but this is about feathers.

Does the efficient function of feathers end here for birds? After all, flight is of primary concern to the bird. No, the proficiency of design goes on.

Feathers provide an insulated cover and even shape a bird's body. There are bird-watchers worldwide who invest in binoculars and expensive cameras just to capture the beauty of the birds' definitive colors. Those handsome feathers serve as displays in courtship and mating rituals as well.

As is true with most design, we observe in all the earth and space that there is an awesome conception of extreme efficiency. And always, there is the artistic touch that rouses our emotions to enjoy that magnificent engineering even if we never know anything but how pretty it is.

BUG OIL MOSQUITO REPELLANT

I have always marveled at inventions. I try to imagine the first person trying something completely unheard of before—not improvement ideas—brand new ideas.

For instance, there were many medicines thousands of years ago. Some were dangerous, some useless and others worked very well. Without the results being written down, translated and read, others could not benefit from the knowledge gained.

Thousands of years ago, who said, "Let me take this leaf and boil it to make tea" and then afterwards said, "Hey, this tea helped my headache go away"?

Every single medicine and invention was a total experiment at some point in time. It seems like plenty of folks would have been poisoned in the process of experimenting, with eating so many things in the woods.

One of the reasons so many scientific fields have accelerated their progress is the sharing of information through publications and, more recently, the internet.

Okay, I said all that to say I read in *Ripley's Believe It or Not* that the Madagascar Lemur uses the poison from giant millipedes as an insect repellent on its body. First of all, a Lemur is a furry, tree-hopping creature from an island off the southeast coast of Africa. Actually, it is a primate (a monkey).

Now if I was in the woods and plagued with mosquitoes, chances are I would not think of squeezing any bug and rubbing it on my skin as a bug repellent. By chance, I might use the wrong bug and attract mosquitoes, a brown bear or have an allergic reaction.

Did some Lemur experiment with different bugs and "bingo!" discover "Hey, this really works"? Even if that were true fellow Lemurs would never know about it because Lemurs don't publish things or even talk. Okay then, the Lemur must communicate this bug-juice discovery to other Lemurs starting with the family and the local community and ultimately to the entire Lemur species as well as to every generation yet unborn.

Not an easy task. So how does the Lemur solve this problem? Maybe he just realized that the only surefire way to do that would be to put that knowledge into his own DNA. This way the whole species would benefit.

Well, as far as we know nobody else has figured out how to do this but obviously, somebody knows how because all the Lemurs know about the bug repellent. There are untold numbers of beneficial instincts, both discovered and not discovered, in life forms from one-celled organisms, fishes, vegetation, to reptiles and mammals.

Okay, so who knows how to do what obviously is being done without us humans knowing how? Because I still don't know which bug to smear on me to keep away other bugs. Somebody out there is smarter than we are.

COORDINATING MUTATIONS?

Hummingbirds have a poor sense of smell and eyes that detect little color except in the red part of the color range. Of course, we all see the long, slender beak the tiny hummingbirds have. Practically a perfect match with the hummingbird, Fuchsia (pronounced "few-sheea") flowers are colorful flowers relying heavily on hummingbirds for pollination. The sweet smells that are commonly found in flowers to attract other birds are absent in the Fuchsia. Fuchsias have hardly any scent, they are brilliant red, and their sweet nectar is only at the end of its long, slender flower.

While hummingbirds get nectar from flower to flower, the flowers' pollen is spread. Shorter beaked birds can't get the nectar simply because the slender flower is too deep to reach.

To the hummingbird, the world is a black and white except for red things. We have seen slick TV commercials in black and white with just one thing or person having any color. In the same way, the red Fuchsia stands out as the only color in a hummingbird's vision even if surrounded by bright blue, purple, yellow and green.

It is as though the Fuchsia and the hummingbird were made for each other. One encyclopedia I read does not call this a "match made in heaven" but credits this process to "co-evolution." Ha! Let me explain "co-evolution" to you.

It is already crazy to believe an amoeba continually mutated into every species that now exists and then coded DNA to stop mutating so species could protect their current form. Co-evolution suggests two separate species coordinate their miraculous and permanently DNA coded evolution.

Let me dramatize co-evolution with a short, little play. I introduce to you four characters: a bird, a flower, and each of their individual DNAs. They all have the ability to converse with each other.

Let's go way back before the hummingbird and the Fuchsia flower "co-evolved." Imagine this cartoonish 4-way meeting BEFORE the hummingbird and Fuchsia flower "evolved" into what they are today.

PRIMITIVE HUMMINGBIRD-TO-BE; SPEAKING TO A FLOWER: *"I'm so little. I can't compete with all these big birds. I need help. Is there some kind of deal we can make?*

PRIMITIVE FUCHSIA-TO-BE: *"Well, we would need some promises from you too. We can't afford to risk extinction by giving up all the other birds that help pollinate us and become almost exclusive. Why would we do that just for you?"*

PRIMITIVE HUMMINGBIRD-TO-BE: *"Okay, if you help us, we'll help you. We will pollinate you almost exclusively. And by 'we' I mean my descendents."*

PRIMITIVE FUCHSIA-TO-BE: *"Alright, we'll give up our sweet smell and attract fewer birds. Of course, by 'we', I also mean my descendents."*

PRIMITIVE HUMMINGBIRD-TO-BE: *"Alright, we'll give up our ability to smell so we won't be attracted to the sweet smell of other flowers."*

PRIMITIVE FUCHSIA-TO-BE: *"Okay. And we'll give up our blue and yellow varieties and go mostly red. That's the best I can offer."*

PRIMITIVE HUMMINGBIRD-TO-BE: *"Great and we'll even give up seeing all colors except red."*

PRIMITIVE FUCHSIA-TO-BE: *"Alright, I like that. Now we're talking. I will try just one more thing; how about we grow longer petals so it's hard to reach inside to keep short-beaked birds from getting our nectar. Can you grow longer beaks?"*

PRIMITIVE HUMMINGBIRD-TO-BE: *"Great idea! We'll do it. Of course, none of this matters unless our DNA can do it and is willing to."*

HUMMINGBIRD-TO-BE'S DNA: *"You don't know what you're asking! This will take millions, maybe billions of years."*

PRIMITIVE HUMMINGBIRD-TO-BE: *"But can you do it?"*

HUMMINGBIRD-TO-BE'S DNA: *"Yes I can do it, but what good is it if the flower DNA can't pull this off on their end?"*

FUCHSIA'S DNA: *"What, are you kidding? You think you can work wonders with your bird and we can't work with this flower. Of course we can do it. Probably in just a couple hundred thousand years."*

HUMMINGBIRD-TO-BE'S DNA: *"Wait a minute. That's right. Listen bird, if the flower gets deep before we have designed and created long beaks we won't even be able to get the nectar! That would be a disaster! Extinction! We would sabotage our own existence!"*

FUCHSIA'S DNA: *"Okay, Okay. We'll have to coordinate better. Let's synchronize our clocks to make sure we don't accidentally make each other extinct. We absolutely must change at the same time for this to work."*

HUMMINGBIRD-TO-BE'S DNA: *"How about we target completed evolution in 300,000 years but check with each other every 50,000 years to stay on track? Are we in agreement on this?"*

EVERYONE: *"Right!"*

You think this is silly? I hope you do. I do too. Maybe it took fantastic intelligence. I'm having a hard time buying unrelated species coordinating DNA to engineer successful co-evolution between species. But hey, that's me.

Whenever I look at hummingbirds outside our window—the idea of a fantastic, artistic designer sits easy in my mind.

IN THE KITCHEN

Alibrando's Law #8
Orchestration

UN-PROVABLE NOTION: Things accidentally (or naturally) invent themselves to function and interact in a vast, interdependent network requiring no coordination.

SENSIBLE FACT: Coordinated interaction of independent systems requires skilled supervision.

TECHNICAL WORDING: *Integrating independent systems for a cause greater than their independent causes requires a perspective of all systems and the ability to coordinate them.*

The graphic below represents design interacting perfectly with outside systems, proving it is intentionally designed to do so.

Independent systems coordinating with other systems	**=**	Intentional Management

EXPLAINING THE LAW

You can imagine an accident disassembling a jigsaw puzzle. You may have difficulty, however, imagining an accident completely assembling a jigsaw puzzle.

Result-oriented thinking can assemble a jigsaw puzzle. Can an accident?

We are discussing a jigsaw puzzle on a table and I know you get it.

A three dimensional puzzle would be far more complicated; even harder to put together by accident.

Take it up another notch and make the puzzle moving while having various properties and chemical reactions that must be internally and externally arranged.

When I say "arranged" I mean so that every "part" is a different species, plant, living organism, chemical, mineral or element. Each living species has to fit with chemicals, minerals and elements around it so nothing kills it. It must "fit" into its environment. Every single living thing has needs so within that puzzle not only must every living thing "fit" into its environment but everything it needs to live and thrive must also be in the puzzle. Are all the resources for every single piece put there together correctly? It makes any other puzzle look easy.

Let's make a huge puzzle. Not the size of the universe or the world; let's make it bigger than a tabletop though. How about ¼ mile cubed? And let's limit it to say, one million parts. It includes chemicals, scientific properties, elements, atoms, cells, changing weather, bugs, fish, reptiles, plants, dirt, mammals and instincts. Okay, can you put it together so that not one thing lacks what it needs?

You think you might need intelligence to do this puzzle or do you think you could put this together by closing your eyes and just start throwing things? Well, you have it easy. You are working with things that have already been invented. Let's take it up another notch. First invent these one million things and creatures from scratch so they all work and then invent the puzzle. Yeah, you have to invent the pieces. How are you going to put these things together? How many inventions are you going to have to create just to make the puzzle fit? You can't invent just ears; you have to invent sounds and sound waves. You have to invent brains to interpret the sound waves and you have to have the ability to make things and animals make sounds. To have these million pieces fit together you will have to invent untold billions of things to make this work. And don't forget, you can't invent something that helps 200 different species but accidentally destroys another 200 species or something else. It has to all fit and work.

After you have invented all one million parts to flawlessly interact, you must now put it together so it works. But here is the biggest part of the trick. Now that you know how outrageously challenging it is to put this together, you are asked this question:

"What are the chances of all of this being put together by accident instead of by you?"

I'm sure, you don't believe you could put the parts of a wind up clock together by dropping pieces on the floor; but you are being asked if you believe the universe, every living thing, all the planets, stars, gases and chemicals so wonderfully organized in harmony did happen and fit together functioning every moment—by accident.

But for the sake of just helping you understand this law I want you, for this moment, to just consider the incredible feat of making everything in our universe FIT TOGETHER.

Imagine just one million separate things, species and elements disconnected having separate properties each with its own agenda for existence or survival.

Just leave those one million pieces alone and now let's wait for all the pieces to put themselves together.

Even a 5-piece puzzle won't do that.

LAW #8

Integrating independent systems for a cause greater than their independent causes requires a perspective of all systems and the ability to coordinate them.

RELATED ARTICLES:
How Come A Squirrel Has A Heart Like Me?
Coordinating Mutations
Ingenious No-Brain
The Orchestra

THE ORCHESTRA

Let's put together a 100-piece orchestra using 100 skilled musicians that never met. There are far more than 100 different parts of nature that work together in a coordinated way. Certainly, these various species and systems in nature did not first meet in a boardroom and discuss how they will coordinate. Like strangers, each separate species and various systems work strictly for their own benefit, unconscious of other species or systems.

So let's put these various musicians in 100 separate sound-proof rooms each equipped with a microphone feeding into the same recording studio. They are instructed to play whatever they want over the next 8 hours and take breaks whenever they want.

We are recording 100 different soundtracks that will be played back together. Separately, we might get some good stuff but guess what, when you play all 100 tracks at the same time it is an unbearable mess of noise, confusion and discord—anything but music.

What do we need? We need to coordinate these players. Producing good music while beeing unable to hear or meet each other is as unlikely as the DNA from different species meeting for the sake of coordinating.

And how likely is it that DNA from any species can perceive and analyze non-DNA resources such as weather, chemicals, gases in the air, the influence of the seasons, etc?

So we simply tell the musicians to all play the same classical piece, but whenever they want. It's not coordinated very well by the not so wise manager. They may play in different keys, and start at different times. It sounds horrible.

Third try, let's give the musicians sheet music so they are at least playing the same music in the same key and now the manager of this experiment tells them to all start playing at precisely 3pm. We are making progress and it is definitely taking more and more wisdom from a supervisor, but after about one minute it becomes obvious that there are different tempos. Those that started just one second later than others are constantly out of sync with everyone. After two minutes we realize, this too is a failure. It sounds awful.

We need a conductor. We need someone to oversee the tempo from start to finish for a beautiful symphony. All 100 musicians need to be "plugged in" to that one conductor so they can maintain their rightful place in the song; when to stop, when to start, keeping the tempo and whatever other details they need to know that the conductor will tell them. Naturally, this is all useless if any musician refuses to do what the conductor commands.

Does anyone on the planet really know how simple coordinating a 100-piece orchestra for one song is, compared to coordinating all of life on earth? To coordinate all life, systems, chemicals, orbits around the sun, tides, weather, DNA, cells, atoms, elements and animal instincts to all work in a perfectly seamless interdependence on more levels than any scientist can even measure? If this isn't monumental enough, this has been working every day from the origins of all the species and systems to right now, and still continues.

Yeah. Our world, all of nature, the universe—what an orchestration!

The Biggest

We love to see big things. Contests, published accounts… bring it on. The biggest tomato, the biggest pumpkin, the biggest man or woman, even the largest ball of string in the world is a tourist attraction. We would not be so attracted to dinosaurs if they were small creatures. It intrigues us to imagine such huge creatures walking among us.

The Brachiosaurus was, according to current records, probably the largest of the dinosaurs weighing up to 50 tons. However, to date, the biggest living creature known to man is no dinosaur, but the whale; particularly the blue whale. I am talking big. One hundred feet long may not sound big until you start comparing it to something smaller like the Tyrannosaurus Rex, which was about twenty feet tall and forty feet long. The Blue Whale's heart weighs about 1,000 lbs. and is the size of a Volkswagen beetle. A person could crawl through the aorta. Whales weigh about 120 tons, nearly three times more than a Brachiosaurus. Just the weight of a blue whale's blood is 7 tons. That is 14,000 pounds of blood circulating. The largest whale ever weighed was 190 tons. The tongue alone weighed about 4 tons.

Although immense, they are not big blobs. They are more sophisticated than any nuclear submarine, outfitted with design inside and out to literally live in the oceans, socialize, eat, digest, hunt, reproduce, swim and ward off enemies in ways only a genius inventor could imagine and a genius engineer could design.

Blue whales eat about 3.5 to 4 tons of food a day.

Adults eat krill (like little shrimp) by getting underneath them and climbing rapidly. When they open their mouth very wide it acts like brakes and the whales basically stop. They open their mouths so wide their jaws disarticulate (disconnect) like snakes do when they eat big stuff. They scoop up a bunch of krill then spit out the water through the baleen that acts like a screen. A typical diet of 4 tons a day has the calorie equivalent of 12,000 hamburgers.

Baby whales drink 50–200 pounds of milk each day. How many dairy cows would we have to milk in one day to bottle 200 pounds of milk? I will have to remember to ask a dairyman.

A single whale calf is born every two or three years to a fertile female whale. Newborns weigh in at about 2.5 tons but some articles say they can weigh as much as 5 tons. Mama's milk is squirted in pretty big squirts. Each squirt could fill a bathtub. Yep, about 33 gallons! That nursing goes on for about six months. That's gotta be a lotta milk.

Life spans are controversial ranging from 30 years to 80–90 years.

They can dive for 5 to 20 minutes and usually go to depths of 490 feet but, can go deeper.

When they surface, they make a huge sound which is the exhale and inhale. While humans exchange about 10–15% of their air capacity per breath, a whale exchanges 80–90% in just one breath using its 1 ton lungs.

They swim at a speed of 19 mph when being chased, but usually swim much slower.

They have no teeth but rather baleen; 320 pairs of black baleen plates in the mouth.

These guys are also the loudest animal on earth. A power saw is about 110 dB (decibels), threshold of pain to the human ear is 120–130 dB, a jet engine is 140 dB, peak of amplified rock music is 150 dB. The whale calls are very loud at 188 dB. Their sounds travel many miles underwater.

They stay warm with a 2–14 inch layer of blubber.

The blue whales have two blow holes. The whales blow shoots 40–50 feet above the surface of the water. A child could crawl through one of those blow holes.

Blue whales frequently swim in pairs.

So imagine it is you who is given the task to design a creature that can do what a whale does. First, let's decide what materials to use. Our materials should seal out water and be sleek enough to slide easily through the water. The structure must be strong enough to endure water pressure at depths of 500 feet. What will propel our machine? What will we use for fuel? How often will we need to refuel? What heating and cooling system shall we use? In our world travels we will be in both cold and warm waters.

The whale is enveloped with a thick layer of fat that helps not only to keep this mammal warm in frigid waters but also to float effortlessly. In warm waters, they can release heat by controlling blood flow to the skin. Its skin is smooth and feels like smooth, wet rubber. The neck has 80–100 furrows that alternately expand and contract to take in and push out water. This, my friend, is some fine technology.

Only an estimated 6,000 to 14,000 live today. During the 1930–31 whale hunting season, about 30,000 blue whales were killed.

If they become extinct, frankly, we could never invent one. We just don't have the knowledge. And if someone says it was designed by accident with no purpose or intelligence, that's just a whale of a story.

Dog-gone Interesting

I love my dog. I could just go on about her but then I'd use up the article bragging.

All dogs have some similarities but no two are exactly alike. Of the dogs I've owned since childhood, they all have a few unique characteristics. What a fantastic invention. We put up with the shedding hair. We deal with ridding our pets of fleas, ticks and any other ailments.

They manage to survive eating nearly anything because they have a very aggressive liver. While our liver has two lobes, theirs has six lobes.

Dogs have great hearing. Humans can hear about 20,000 vibrations a second while dogs can hear 35,000 vibrations a second, nearly twice as good. More amazing is their ability to shut off their inner ear to filter out distracting sounds. I wish I could do that. Of course, I can filter out certain requests at home when asked.

Humans actually see better than dogs in the bright of day, but dogs see better than us at night. They have a third eyelid, but I still don't know why.

Did you ever notice how oblivious new born pups are? Those really cute puppies that seem so out of it are out of it because they are born blind and deaf. That's got to help with long naps.

Dogs have an acute sense of smell but not taste. I won't mention the gross stuff my dog has been yelled at for eating. According to articles I've read, dogs will eat almost anything if they are hungry and rarely chew their food unless it is dry and crunchy.

Just like us, they have baby teeth replaced by adult teeth and their number is also very precise. 28 baby teeth erupt by 6–8 weeks but by the time they are 6–7 months old, they have replaced all 28 baby teeth with 42 adult teeth. They are named "canine" after their teeth.

Dogs have 319 bones, unless the tail is absent...

Humans have 78 pairs or chromosomes but dogs have 39. That is 39 chromosomes whether it is a Poodle, a Labrador, German shepherd, Great Dane, Chihuahua, Collie or mutt.

But obviously, this is not what we love about dogs, at least those that do love dogs. It is their personality, their companionship, how they make us smile or laugh out loud.

I have had some favorite dogs in my life. The dog I have now and her mother are two of my favorites. But all dogs have certain characteristics universally. Almost anyone can talk about what they love about their dog and other dog owners start relating and want to talk about their own dog(s).

As soon as my dog sees me or hears my voice, she begins wagging her tail.

This is part of the dog "personality." What a cool invention. It's fun. I like it. The way they open their mouth like a smile and wag their tail is great

The way they instantly respond to the tone of our voice; first they wag their tail but if you say "No, bad!" the dog lowers her head, puts her tail between her legs, crouches a little and looks up to see what you are going to do next. Then you say, "Good girl!" in a happy voice and instantly she wags her tail, lifts her head and maybe tries to lick you. She doesn't know why she was in trouble sometimes or why she is off the hook but she never gets moody about things. She is immediate in her response, even if you go back and forth.

"Good girl, bad girl, good girl." Of course, it is our tone of voice, not our words.

If your dog is young enough, occasionally they get all hyper and decide to just run like crazy in large, sprinting circles. It cracks me up.

Mine loves to play ball. She also likes to play nab the feet of my son, in a type of wrestling with him, which she has really enjoyed since she was a pup. He brings her in the house and takes off his shoes but leaves his socks on and starts pushing her around. Then she knows it's time to bite on his feet while he spins around trying to keep his feet away from her. She jumps over him or runs in circles and always gets his feet. I smile just thinking about it.

I think something that every human master enjoys about his or her dog is how the dog is almost always glad to see you.

With satellite TV, I surf the channels looking for entertainment. A satellite in space, millions of dollars in entertainment production costs, billions of advertising dollars and the cost of TV technology are all to entertain me. Some days I could just use a laugh. I click from channel to channel. I see so many shows with canned laughter so I know when I am supposed to laugh. But truthfully, my pets probably make me smile more. Hey, I know they are just animals, but the pleasure I derive from my pets is undeniable.

I shake my head when I hear how many billions of dollars are spent on pets in America when there is so much human need, but they become a part of the family. It's kind of strange but I understand it because of my own pets. I guess it is the interaction. I know them and they know me.

It is not merely some invention of wondrous engineering. It is a species with whom we find ourselves having a relationship. We are saddened by their death. We find comfort in making these creatures happy. Our eyes meet and I wonder what she is thinking, really. And as she wags her tail, I appreciate the fact that I know she isn't really concerned with what I am thinking about or going through, only that I am happy with her. Our dogs seem to take pleasure in pleasing us.

How do you invent such a thing as a dog?

DNA

DNA—Supreme Beings?

Much of the specific numbers regarding DNA are taken from: *LIFE'S KEY-DNA by Marleen Maley Hutchins c1961 The National Foundation published by Coward-McCann, Inc.*

With paternity cases, we hear about DNA. Genetic DNA coding was also featured in the movie, *Jurassic Park*. DNA *is* genetic coding. That means it is the blueprint, the plan for our body.

Like a construction project on a house, every contractor gets a copy of the same blueprint with different parts highlighted for them to do. The house dimensions are the same for the concrete man, the plumber, the electrician, the bricklayer, the roofer, etc.

In a similar way, the DNA from any kind of cell in a person will reveal the same person. We see getting DNA samples now on crime scene investigations. It doesn't matter if it is a blood sample, a hair, a piece of a fingernail or saliva; they all identify the same person. Blood has a very different job description than hair or saliva but they all work for one exclusive employer—the person—the very unique individual who's entire network of all different kinds of cells with different jobs.

We are unique and our DNA coding, the master plan for each of us, is in every cell of our body—*every cell in your body*. That is about 10 trillion cells (13 zeros after the one).

There is supposed to be (get ready for this) 6 feet of DNA packed into each cell, if you laid it out lengthwise.

Are you getting what I am saying? Six feet of DNA in each one of your 10 trillion cells!

I am not six feet tall but I have 6 feet of DNA packed real tight in every one of my cells!

You could stretch out your own DNA all the way to the moon… all the way to the moon and back… all the way to the moon and back more than 20,000 times! How's that for miniaturization?

It has been determined that DNA coding is responsible for preserving the ongoing character of every cell of every living organism of every single species of every plant and animal on earth. Think about that for just a minute.

In your mother's womb your DNA code said you were to be human, how tall you would be, what color eyes you would have, whether you would have dimples or not, if you would be hairy or not, whether you would have cute or ugly toes, short or long eyelashes, dark complexion or freckles, be male or female, and so on. This was all there once the egg was fertilized. It is just an amazing building process after that.

But, pay attention, the DNA from mom and dad started out as just two cells; *one* from dad and *one* from mom. All the cells in your body have forty-six chromosomes (the coding) but not these two cells. No, they each have only twenty-three chromosomes until they merge totaling forty-six.

These two lonely cells get real power when they get together. Instead of those two cells reproducing themselves, they begin dictating what the next cells are to become. Some cells are directed to form eyeballs while others become brain cells. Others are told to create bone cells while still other cells form your heart.

From these two original cells comes the design and manufacture of the nervous system, circulatory system, skeletal system, respiratory system, immune system, digestive system, temperature regulation, touch, taste, smell, sight, and hearing, and the brain; with all these systems interdependently working together.

The DNA in those original two little cells commanded all the rest of the cells to become exactly what they are today. Ever since, bone cells have been reproducing only bone cells and brain cells—brain cells, muscle cells, tissue cells, white blood cells, nerves, hair, eyes, nails, teeth, hearing and everything in you, reproducing after its own kind of cell.

Can scientists dictate to cells what to become? Of course not, if they could, they could command cells to create eye cells and form a perfectly functioning eye or anything else they wanted. They are trying to capture and manipulate this process, but they themselves cannot command cells.

Scientists don't have the authority or knowledge to do what they already know DNA can do. They can only experiment with moving DNA and hope it will do what they expect.

So much of the public thinks scientists can do practically anything. The scientists themselves are aware of how very little they truly understand. They only try to manipulate systems that are already here, *not* create new ones.

There is order in DNA so much greater than man can create he can barely even understand its range of power.

How Come A Squirrel Has A Heart Like Me?

The idea of hearing ability in people, dogs, bugs, whales, squirrels and every single species on earth is interesting. But consider this question in light of the evolutionary theory: Did one ear evolve in one species, and then somehow distribute a diagram to all the other creatures that now have ears… or did every species individually have its own version of hearing ears evolve coincidentally, ending with an almost identical design?

It seems more logical that each species developed its own version of hearing. But can you imagine an evolution convention with booths? One for the latest evolutionary blueprints for eyeballs, one for nervous systems, one for blood, one for DNA, another for hair and still another for skeletal material. Because let's face it, there are tremendous similarities straight across the board.

This whole idea puts a tremendous challenge upon the flawed theory of evolution. It would make more sense that each species developed its own version of all specific abilities, ears included, than it does that different species share information for evolving. Don't you agree? So, the screaming question is "How come so many unrelated species seem to share similar or identical 'technologies'?"

How is it that the ear drum idea is shared among humans, lizards, dolphins, squirrels, and thousands of bird species? Did they use the internet?

Does DNA send out a spy to copy good ideas and bring them back to its own species? Not likely.

We use bones to study the past and make grand claims about evolution. Does anyone notice the whole idea that all these old skeletons uniformly had bone marrow and similar technology in joints and cartilage? This is strikingly consistent among most species in ALL time periods?

To me, the evidence points to a *common manufacturer.*

The chlorophyll idea in so many different plants seems more than coincidence.

It is similar to Bill Gates setting up Windows as an operating system and so many programs coincidentally running compatibly on Windows.

It is not a coincidence. It is a thought out design program platform. After Windows came out, thousands of programs have been designed to work on that Windows platform. Wouldn't it be too weird if someone wrote programs that worked on Windows 95 in 1959? That would be a very unlikely feat. Carefully consider the undeniable reality of the beautiful blend of coordinated technology in all nature.

The technology of a blood circulation system with a heart is not something that exists in just humans and monkeys or even just mammals. It is birds and fish too. Whose uniform technology is this?

Let's say every creature on earth that has a heart and blood circulatory system has to pay you a penny a year. Now you would be willing to count how many creatures have a heart because if you can collect a penny a year from every one of them, you'd be filthy rich, even more than Bill Gates! It is a much larger program platform that all of nature works with.

The heart and blood circulation system is a good design but not passed on from one species to a completely different species. For so many different species to have the same or strikingly similar heart/blood circulation design, I'd say is just more evidence of intelligent planning. Then again, millions believe it was just billions of accidents that just happen to have turned out better than anything we can even dream of duplicating with billions of dollars of research.

ART & FRED, THE FISHES

Once upon a time, there was a fish named Art. He was a smart fish and he noticed many of his species would be eaten because they had no camouflage. He had never heard the word "camouflage" before but he talked it over with his friend Fred. Fred, another fish, immediately agreed it was much too easy to be spotted and eaten. Smart Art thought if fish could have lines on them so they could blend in with weeds and sticks that would help—very creative thinking for a fish—especially if one line would go right over the eye. Yeah, and also put a painting of an eye on the tail. That way when fish eaters would attack the painted eye they would think they were attacking the head. They would be expecting the fish to swim forward, not knowing the head is the tail. Boy, this is one reverse strategy thinking fish here. Yeah, that would be great. The fish would go the opposite direction from what the fish eater expected. Art loved his idea.

But Fred the fish had a criticism; *"What if there are no sticks or weeds around?"* He smiled a fishy smile because Fred had an entirely different idea. *"What if a whole bunch of us all stuck together with black and white stripes? Together, we would all look like sticks and the fish eater wouldn't see our shape. He'd think he was seeing just sticks. If a fish eater got too close to us we would all scatter."*

Art disagreed and liked his own idea better. But they had a bigger problem. How could they possibly put their idea in motion? They had already evolved enough to be inventive geniuses and could be military generals today. But what about engineering their ideas? They would have to invent an entirely new species and make it so the species reproduced their ideas without even thinking about it. Wow, big task. And Fred felt his newly invented species would have to stay in school to learn how to stick together and scatter the right way. How to do it, how to do it?

"I've got it!" said Art. No wait a minute, fish don't talk. Ah who cares, on with the story.

Art whispered his idea to Fred so they tried it. They both closed their eyes and wished their babies would have these new ideas planted into their genes by DNA. They wished really, really, really hard. Then they wished that the DNA would not change after that but lock in their design ideas and instincts forever. They didn't know how to change the color of scales or implant subconscious instincts, but guess what? Art's babies became what are now called the Chelmon Rostratus species. They all have stripes and almost always have one right over each eye. They also have what looks like an eye on both sides of their tails, even larger than their real eyes. Fred's babies became the first Damselfishes. Damselfishes are striped with no fake eye but travel in large schools and create camouflage as a group looking like sticks, just like Fred had hoped. Way to go Art and Fred!

The story of Art and Fred is no fairy tale. It is a "scientific" theory that should be a fairy tale. Most scientists will tell you, it took no outside intelligence to design many species of fish that can hide, change colors, and blend with sand, coral, or plants, while others even look like plants or other things. Oh yeah, they will credit "random accidents" which is "random luck" when things turn out well. Fish needed that stuff to survive so "Bingo!" there it is. So if it is always luck without intelligence, it is always "dumb luck."

Even a dumb fish is smarter than dumb luck, so I think the "Art and Fred" theory makes more sense than the dumb luck theory—unless we prefer the theory that intelligent design requires intelligence.

WHO SAYS IT'S FUNNY?

It has been said, for success one needs a wishbone, a backbone and a funny bone.

What is the unlikelihood of certain features evolving, like humor? Laughing hyenas aren't laughing because something is funny, that is just how they bark.

Our cat purrs when he seems happy. Our dog wags her tail when she is happy.

Monkeys can simulate a smile or even laughing gestures. They are really more like mocking gestures. So what is it monkeys think is funny; slapstick, situation comedy, knock-knock jokes? No one does stand-up comedy for a bunch of monkeys.

This is the point. Who invented laughter? The notion of the first cave-man with a trace of humor before humor evolved is hard to pinpoint scientifically. Imagine the first caveman chuckling in the history of the world. Maybe he sees his wife tripping over a rock and hopping on one foot while holding the painful foot in the other hand. The sight of it does something very strange. The caveman looks at her then smiles and then slightly chuckles out loud at the sight. The other tribesmen look at him in wonder. "Ughh" says one of them, which in this case means, "Yo, what are you doing with that weird face and sound?" Then the humor-evolving caveman says, "Oo-wah, Oo-wah" which means, "I don't know, it felt kinda good inside" and points at his wife. Then as he looks at his wife, she shows annoyance but he pictures her stubbing her toe again in his memory and chuckles again. The surprised tribe makes noises all basically meaning, "Dude, what are you doing?"

Even to this day, the guy who gets the joke is smarter than the ones who don't, so the chuckling caveman must have been the most evolved in the group. He was the only one who got the joke.

Now I have seen babies laugh. That is a delight. Why they laugh is something of a mystery but generally parents (or grandparents) prolong the moment as long as possible, repeating whatever gesture makes that baby laugh over and over again until after ten, twenty, or thirty times, the baby finally doesn't think it's funny anymore.

On the other hand, there are things people laugh at that I don't think is funny because I think I'm "more evolved." This includes a whole bunch of TV shows written by professional writers using canned laughter as a cue that something is supposed to be funny that just isn't.

But getting back to the point, what suddenly made a creature think someone stubbing their toe was funny? What makes a baby laugh? The scientific question is what DNA change was so important to the survival of man that the DNA did something as radical as alter itself permanently to infuse into an entire species a sense of humor?

Humor is a big part of human character. We like to laugh. It seems the opposite of sadness. Prolonged sadness or stress seems to affect our health. Laughter brings relief. Studies show laughter also improves health. It is a wonderful invention but I just don't see how DNA could have invented it unless… DNA had a sense of humor before we did. I also can't picture a crowd of DNA strands sharing jokes.

Humor and laughter are too wonderful to have been invented by someone or something that didn't already know the pleasure of laughter. For some chemical or simple life form to accidentally create something like a sense of humor or laughter when it never existed before is not even funny.

THE HUMAN BODY

NATURAL INTELLIGENCE

What do we call it when our bodies seem smarter than us?

I don't know how my heart knows to keep beating rhythmically in proportion to the strain of my body. I don't fully understand how my blood brings oxygen to my cells and takes impurities out. I know I have a brain and a nervous system but really, I don't understand how they work.

The entire medical profession in America actually knows very little about how to heal. Truly, it is the body that heals itself. Do you think we have a headache from an aspirin deficiency? The aspirin does not heal. Aspirin creates a teaspoon of blood in the stomach. That's why aspirin numbs most pain anywhere except in the stomach. Because the body prioritizes its concern to the greatest ailment, in the case of aspirin it thinks it is internal bleeding. A wonder drug? I wonder.

There are many systems inside of our bodies fighting poisons, foreign substances, unwanted bacteria and viruses; and many back up plans in case "Plan A" is not working.

As medical research continues, we learn more about awesome, intricate, clever, brilliant ways your body heals itself and strives for health even though we keep pumping it with preservatives, drugs, foreign chemicals and "food" that not only does not nourish, but literally poisons us.

This is not a commercial on dieting or natural food. This commentary highlights the wonder of superior wisdom dwelling in our own bodies. Very few of us are even aware of all the marvelous, cooperating, interdependent, complex systems within us. Multi-layered systems engineered to give us strength, coordination, eyesight, growth, healing, pleasure, health, reproduction, temperature control, thought-processing, memory, emotions, detoxification, manual dexterity, mobilization, warning systems, survival modes, the instinct to nurture our young, hearing and on and on...

Most of us cannot even name all our anatomical parts that HAVE been discovered and named. We are even more limited in discussing how they all function and interact. All of science has comprehended very little of the intelligence of how these systems work.

Science is still largely at the observation stage of *reporting* what they see, more than truly understanding what they see, in biology.

We can make trains, planes, cars, TVs and computers but when we step into the field of biology, we haven't even reached kindergarten level.

We can transplant. We can manipulate genes and DNA. We can stretch and transfuse. However, we cannot totally manufacture any of it with lasting success, even to this day.

How functional is a picture of a clock on the wall? It's non-functional; for looks only.

That's the cutting edge of biological manufacture at this time… glass eyes, plastic skin and other things that simply *look like* the natural biological image.

Mankind's inability to manufacture biologically from the ground up proves how extremely primitive our science is in contrast to the vast intelligence residing in all living things.

We are still looking for the "miracle cure" for baldness.

The attempt to simply expand certain portions of a woman's figure became a health disaster with Dow Chemical running for bankruptcy.

This is no slap to science, but rather an appeal to the reader to be inspired by the colossal wisdom that still far surpasses all science dwelling right here in each of our very own bodies. Whether or not science knows about or understands all the systems at work inside of us, we freely benefit from its wisdom anyway.

Babies marvelously form in wombs, sometimes undetected for months.

Toxins are removed while we keep putting more toxins into ourselves.

Wounds heal.

Cells are replenished.

I, for one, am thankful that we can see, hear, smell, touch, and taste, whether we understand how it works or not.

Body Stats

We pay big money for insurance. Accidents are bad things that can happen to any of us. Auto collisions, house fires, falling, explosions, floods, high winds and any number of things cause destruction

Amazingly, accidents are a big part of evolution's explanation for how our bodies have been designed. It is that theory's explanation for how the stars and space came into being. "By accidents" is the response to the question, "How did all these living creatures get so marvelously designed?"

Just the design of our human bodies is more than all the medical specialists in the world can even fully understand, let alone repair. We have about 206 bones, though we are born with 305, some fuse. We have 650 muscles and more than 100 joints. We have 60,000 miles of blood traffic (circulatory system). We carry 10 gallons of water in us, amounting to almost two-thirds of our body. In an average lifetime, we breathe approximately 500,000,000 times until our last breath. We have enough fat to make only seven cakes of soap and enough lime to whitewash one small shed. To respond to the pleasure of taste we are equipped with 9,000 taste buds. Then to interpret everything from pain to pleasure, hot to cold, soft to rough, and sharp to blunt, we have nerve cells—13 billion of them (13,000,000,000). We have enough phosphorus to make 2,200 matches. All the hairs all over our bodies actually last only about three years. On the average we have about 5 million hairs. I know that chemically, we are rather inexpensive units.

Your muscles have the aid of tendons to connect them to bones. Those tendons have been tested to withstand a stress of eight tons per square inch.

We do need to consume fuel though. Again, in the average lifetime a person gulps down approximately 50 tons of food; that amounts to 100,000 pounds. That's a lot of calories we burn off. We drink about 11,000 gallons of liquid.

You could buy everything you need to put a human body together for probably under $50. But to put it together so that it works, 900 billion dollars would not be enough because the sophistication of design is so exceedingly above our knowledge. On the other hand, according to the mainstream theories of evolution all you really need is a whole bunch of accidents until everything works.

We have specialists in so many fields of medicine. If just one thing goes wrong there is an incredible amount of knowledge needed in every area.

Our bodies are carefully wrapped in a well-fitted waterproof covering. We have 20 square feet of skin that replaces itself every few weeks. It can heal, warm you with goose bumps, stretch and shrink with weight changes and has 4,000,000 actual nerves for touch.

If accidents can do all these wonderful things, we don't need insurance, we need more accidents… or hey, maybe it's not such a great theory.

CIRCULATE THIS!

Your circulatory system pumps 10 pints of blood EVERY MINUTE, 30 pints per minute during brisk exercise. So while relaxed, your dependable heart keeps pumping approximately 75 gallons of blood every hour or 1,800 gallons per day. That's 12,600 gallons a week or more than 50,000 gallons every month of your life. That is some pump! Every month, your heart is pumping far more volume than it would take to fill a huge built-in swimming pool. How many water pumps out there have a 10 million gallon warranty? NONE. That's what your heart must pump if it quits just at middle age.

I guess we have yet to design such a marvel. Even that bunny that "keeps on going" won't last that long.

Your blood isn't going through a tube and back. It is traveling through a vast network of your own blood vessels, miles worth. How many miles— more than 50 miles—or more than 100 miles? Imagine walking 100 miles to follow your own blood vessels, but it's more than that. It is more than 1,000 miles! How do they all fit inside you? Truthfully, it is so long that I hesitate to tell you just how long it really is. Okay, Okay, I'll tell you. It is more than 10,000 miles long—right there in your own body. That's from Fresno, California to New Jersey, back to Fresno then to Florida and up to New York. Is that possible? That's quite a distance and quite a sophisticated invention, some slick miniaturizing and your very own circulatory system. Some of your capillaries are microscopic and not all are opened at once. It's actually more than 25,000 miles! Oh no, I still haven't admitted how really long your blood circulation system is. If you are an adult you only carry 8–10 pints of blood, about a gallon—that's all. But your blood does so much. It carries the white blood cells to fight all the diseases that want to beat you up. Is a million a large number of white blood cells? How about 50 million? Well, you have more than a billion; 25 billion to quote the scientists! When you move your muscles, you need oxygen there. That is the job of the red blood cells. You have— gulp!—more than 25 billion of those, way more. You have 25 trillion in the gallon or so of blood that your heart is so faithfully pumping through more than 25,000 miles of blood vessels. OK, I'll tell you how really long all your blood vessels are, 60,000 miles. That's the truth. Some design, huh? Amazingly, the sophisticated design of your own bloodstream has 60,000 miles of arteries, veins, and capillaries.

Your 25 trillion (25,000,000,000,000) oxygen-carrying blood cells live about 120 days. It's lucky for you they have the technology of reproduction because it would be real hard to keep building and injecting 25 trillion of those guys every 120 days to keep you alive. Your 25 billion white blood cells only live about 12 hours. Let's face it 25 billion is no small amount either. Anyway, we aren't smart enough to even know how to make a synthetic red or white blood cell that works, let alone miniaturize it and reproduce it at such a high rate or any rate at all.

What designed this? What produces it, tells it when to produce it and how much? And how do all those blood vessels know where to go, what to do, and how to do it? Is there any reasonable theory that claims it was not designed by some incredible intelligence? Amazingly, yes, there is the main theory that this was all done without intelligence and by accident. Now what do you say to that?

You can't call something smart and at the same time say it takes no brains to do it.

In The Kitchen
Alibrando's Law #9
Order Requires Intelligence

Un-provable Notion: Designs in nature are not related to intelligence but rather results of many random accidents over billions of years.

Sensible Fact: It always takes brains to fix something, organize something new, or make something better.

Technical Wording: *Order and design are always an indication of intelligence.*

The graphic below represents the relationship between intelligence and working design.

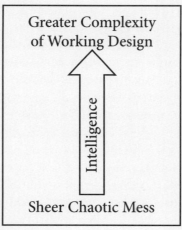

It is simple to understand that the more complex a design or invention is the more intelligence is required to design it. Whenever we see design, we are looking at intelligence. Whenever man attempts to imitate natures design, intellegence is required. There are no *provable* exceptions to this law.

LAW #9

> *Order and design are always an indication of intelligence.*

RELATED ARTICLES:
Nearly every article in this book

BIONIC WANNA-BE

Everyone pretty much figures that our science people can do just about anything. I'm impressed with jets, TVs, computers, and how make-up can really help some women.

They can even make a glass eye that looks *so* real. It looks real but it doesn't look at all, if you know what I mean. I mean it can't see. The whole science of bionics just proves how little we really know.

Anybody remember the bionic "Six-Million Dollar Man"? That was fantasy science-fiction. Bionics is the science of imitating natural things. At the end of one of the Star Wars movies, Luke Skywalker had a new mechanical hand to replace the old human one. Sure, seemed easy enough.

Think of the technology necessary to replace your own hand; heat detectors so you don't melt the "skin," "skin" that can heal itself. Both of these are already beyond the grasp of science. You would also need motor controls "extraordinaire," so you can play a piano, a guitar, a harp, or tighten tiny screws for your glasses or earphones. Gotta have millions of sensory cells all connected to your real nervous system so you can tell the difference between soft tissue paper and the stuff that will scratch up your nose in a day; sensitive enough to feel the soft fur of a kitten and the right pair of socks in the dark. Your hands are strong enough to swing a hammer and if you rake too much—grow calluses. Your bionic hands must be watertight enough to do dishes and wash yourself too.

Hold your hand wide open and look at your palm. Your four fingers are all different lengths. Now keeping your hand open, just bend all four fingers down. Your fingertips now all line up. That's some symmetry you probably didn't notice before.

The fake hand should be able to detect cold too. You want to know when to put them in your pockets before they freeze.

We need fingers to clean our ears, check our shave, tickle somebody, button our shirts, pull up our socks; c'mon… bionics is nowhere close.

Don't forget, the fingers have to be able to "snap" to the music. It should be a song of thanks for the wonder of our wonderful hands. Forget the snap, applause is better.

HAIR MATTERS

I'm told human heads have about 150 hairs per square inch. I learned this while visiting the Lawrence Hall of Science at the University of California, Berkeley with Big Creek School students.

The tour guide told us why dogs can play and take naps so comfortably in the snow. They have 60,000 hairs per square inch. A pretty big jump—150 per inch to 60,000. If they had only 100 times more hair per square inch, that would be 15,000 hairs. Dogs have 400 times as much hair per square inch as we do. It seems impossible.

We were actually viewing two life size sculptures of elephant seals, which was the topic at hand. The tour guide then disclosed that the seals had about 1 million hairs per square inch! In addition to the fat, these hairs enable the elephant seal to keep warm in the frigid waters. That is more than 6,500 times as much hair as humans have per square inch. I really can't even conceive this.

He continued telling us that the longest observed length of time for these mammals staying underwater was two hours although the average was closer to 50 minutes.

These amazing features were slighter than the astonishing fact that elephant seals can dive down an entire mile under water.

Here we have a creature that can go about 5,000 feet underwater without being crushed by the pressure or its eyes popping out. They can then rise quickly without getting the bends all while holding its breath as long as 2 hours.

Our scientists or military would love to duplicate this technology. What if they could alter you so you could hold your breath for just 30 minutes and go underwater to 500 feet comfortably?

Like you, these seals have no gills. If they could conduct surgery on you so you would have these abilities by this summer, boy could you show off.

The Navy Seals could also make great use of a team with these abilities on military missions.

Well, the technology really is right in front of us with these elephant seals. Unfortunately, the design, like most of nature, is so advanced they still can't figure it out—even while looking right at it.

Scientists can poke and slice, look under microscopes, perform experiments, run info through computers for analysis and frequently end up feeling tricked by some master magician. The sheer intelligence of such systems continues to have the upper hand on scientists. Scientists can only marvel at how great it would be if they could figure it out and applaud at being so well fooled.

If they could figure how to just get human hair to 150 per square inch for some of us guys with thinning hair, they'd make multi-millions or billions. Ah, if only…

Miracle Slow-grow

In a recent conversation, a barber in Madera said he has imagined for years inventing a tonic that would slow the hair from growing. If he put it on a customer's head right after the haircut, the haircut could last six months. The customer wouldn't need a haircut for six months but for him to not go broke his $12 haircut would have to cost $60 to cover that loss of monthly haircuts. But alas, he just keeps cutting hair.

In a previous article (years ago) I referred to how unusual it is that eyebrows and eyelashes STOP growing at a certain length and the cosmetics industry earns many millions in helping women's eyelashes look $1/16^{th}$ of an inch longer. But one of the very first articles I wrote was called "Growth Gunk" about the inability of science to make anything grow.

But the barber got me thinking about the fortune that could be made in the "stop or slow the growth" industry. Imagine mowing your lawn and putting "SLOW-GROW" on your lawn and having to only mow every three months. The golf courses would save money. This would be bad for the landscapers unless they charged more (like the barber's idea).

Men could rub it on their face and not have to shave for six months. Old guys could put some in their hairy ears and nostrils. Women could put it on their legs (and face, if needed).

Science cannot figure out how to make a garden hose grow or eyelashes stop at a 16th of an inch. So far, we have yet to figure out how to make grass or anything else stop growing without killing it. Right now, the only way we know how to stop real grass from growing is to not water it, but eventually it dies from the lack of water.

Whatever the wisdom that tells eyelashes and eyebrows to stop growing at a certain length probably contains the secrets to making other hair
or grass stop growing. We just don't know what those secrets are. We are
not that smart. If someone figures it out and has the business savvy to
get a patent, they are going to be a billionaire.

Funny how, once a man can figure out how nature does something,
he can get a patent on it and say it is his idea.

So once again, a nod of respect is in order to a greater intelligence
than our own. And if we do ever figure it out, that is no cause to with-
draw that respect.

BAREFOOTIN'

If your feet were frozen and had to be amputated and then technology
offered its best options, you would appreciate the sophistication of those
feet at the end of your legs like never before. As Ben Franklin said, "We
know the worth of water when the well is dry."

The cost of a prosthetic foot makes name brand sneakers look cheap.
Science fiction may present bionics as superior body parts but science *non-
fiction* is quite different. We have more than an ankle joint for a flexible
foot. Our ankle joint is complex enough to offer many tilt options. You
can move your foot in a circular motion in either direction. Your foot has
more than a heel bone, foot bone and five toes. It has twenty-six bones or
fifty-two bones for both feet. Almost half the bones in your entire body
are in your hands and feet. Each foot has not five, ten or fifteen complex
joints, but thirty-three complex joints. Think about the intricacy of twenty-
six bones with thirty-six complex joints. I bet you can't even figure out
how they work in your own feet. All these bones and joints need to move
so you are equipped with more than one hundred ligaments, muscles and
tendons. The ligaments are flexible fiber bands joining your foot bones.
The tendons connect your muscles to the bones. Each one of these has
more amazing technology including the bone matter, bone marrow and
healing abilities. With all this, it still isn't plugged in! The foot is connected to the brain so you can command your foot to move walking up
steps, down a hill or putting your shoes on. It needs to be connected for
reflex actions from our middle ear for balancing through the brain and
those signals must be lightening-quick to prevent us from falling. Don't
forget the nerve network to inform you that you have stubbed your toe,
stepped on a tack or worse. The pain is good incentive to avoid damag-
ing your precious feet. Don't omit the blood circulation to keep your feet
warm. None of this stuff comes with the prosthetic foot.

Each foot actually sweats about a pint of perspiration a day. Whew, no wonder our socks are stinky. There are more sweat glands on the soles of your feet than any other part of your body.

Your feet support the whole rest of your body all your life. On a given day the average person takes 18,000 steps (if you're really bored try counting all your steps in a day). I wonder what it is for couch potatoes. In your lifetime, you walk enough to go around the world three times (75,000 miles). Feet can swell 5–10% bigger by the end of your day.

If you walk barefoot, your skin will thicken for you, this is called calluses. Prosthetics sure don't do that.

Let me put it this way; mankind's technology can send a satellite to Mars that takes pictures. This feat (f-e-A-t) is within our ability. To manufacture feet like the ones you were born with is much farther out of reach than Mars. The design of our feet is sophistication beyond all humanity's scientific ability.

Since we can make a satellite, it would be easier for a picture-taking satellite to evolve than a human foot.

So when you see your own footprints in the dirt this summer, remember it is a better foot than money can buy—funny toes and all.

MUSCLES, GOOD IDEA
656. Not 657, not 655. 656.

Your body, and every other human body on earth, has 656 muscles.

Those muscles are identically separated into two groups: voluntary and involuntary.

That means you don't have to worry that your heart will stop beating if you forget to tell it to beat. These are "involuntary" muscles. Your involuntary muscles are on autopilot and line internal organs (lungs, intestines, blood vessels, heart and even glands).

You may instinctively blink your eyes or scratch your nose, but you can also voluntarily do it anytime. Your voluntary muscles aren't floating but are attached to the skeleton by tendons.

It's interesting that in the so-called evolutionary process, something said "Whoa, stop! This is good right here—656 muscles. We got it covered. Okay, it's a take."

Naturally, according to the theory, no intelligent guide was involved. It's just a process of phenomenal luck (my sarcasm, of course).

The ol' lucky process landed on a good idea by constructing nerves running through all the muscles. It's good because another good idea was

adding the electrical impulses running through those nerves to stimu-
late the muscles to contract. Hey, what luck!

Fortunately, those nerves run all the way to the brain so whenever
the brain decides to move any muscle, it sends those electrical impulses
to the selected muscles.

All muscles, no exceptions, work by shortening—or pulling, never
by pushing.

Another clever idea (wow, how lucky) was the way the muscles *just
happened* to evolve into "teams." You see, every set of muscles has an
opposing set of muscles to reverse motion.

Just think, if only one set of our muscles did not have the opposite
set of muscles, you might scratch your nose, and have to get someone to
put your arm back down. Or maybe you would look to the right and not
have the opposite set to turn your head back straight.

Ah, alas we were real lucky that of all 656 muscles—every one—has
that opposite match and they all have the nerves too. Every one of our
muscles is connected to the brain. All of our muscles equally know how
to replenish themselves with cell reproduction. The muscles all have the
ability to do some minor healing and they all are connected to tendons,
bones, organs or glands. Anybody who thinks all of this could happen
by accident or luck, tell me why multi-million dollar robots designed by
highly trained specialists can't come close to being anything like it.

Remember this article at the next Olympics.

In The Kitchen
Alibrando's Ripple 1 of Law #9
Accidental Implausibility

If you understand Law #9 about order in scale with intelligence, then you
can see how this 1st ripple is following along the same lines, the same
idea. This emphasizes the growing unlikelihood of accidents as a source
of design.

Un-provable Notion: No matter how increasingly intelligent a design
is, it can still happen billions of times by accident.

Sensible Fact: The more complex a design is, the less likely it is to be
made by accident.

TECHNICAL WORDING: *The likelihood of accidental occurrence decreases proportionately with the increase of order.*

Below, the graphic represents how one increase always causes a decrease of the other.

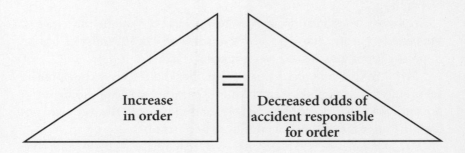

EXPLAINING THE LAW

If you throw two marbles on the ground, you can draw an imaginary line between the two. Naturally, this is a straight line. Actually, a line between any two points is a *straight* line. So 100 times out of 100 times when you drop two marbles on the ground, they lay on the ground in a way that you could draw a straight line between them.

This is not true with three marbles. Most of the time when you simply drop three marbles on the ground they will *not* land with all three in a straight row. Now somewhere, somebody can tell you the chances of getting a straight row by dropping three marbles on the ground. Maybe it is 1:20, let's say it is. It is hard to get three marbles to line up in a row by accident every time but very possible (using my fictional ratio) 1 in 20 times on an average.

Okay, what if we do the same with four marbles. The likelihood of four marbles accidentally lining up into a straight row is much harder than three. Get four rocks or pennies or marbles and try. It certainly is possible, but on an average, it may only happen once in 150 times (another fictional number to make a point). So your chances of getting a straight row with four marbles are 1:150. Do you see a pattern developing here?

By now, you can predict if we try the same thing with five marbles the ratio will increase greatly; maybe something like 1:1000. It gets harder and harder to accidentally organize a row of marbles the more marbles there are. Five marbles is a considerably greater order than two marbles.

If we accelerate to grabbing twenty marbles and throwing them up in the air over and over until all twenty are in a straight row... well, it would be a while. Do you want to try? Me either. It would take too long to happen even once, let alone ten times to come up with an average ratio.

Which is the greatest order, three marbles, ten marbles or twenty marbles? Obviously, twenty marbles is the greatest order and the least likely to occur by accident.

Is there any logic or rational argument to dispute this fact? Using experimentation and the scientific method, it is undisputable.

RIPPLE 1 OF LAW #9

> *The likelihood of accidental occurrence decreases proportionately with the increase of order.*

RELATED ARTICLES:
Just Luck

HEALING SKIN

Did you ever tell someone about the really bad scrape you got and when you went to show him/her the scar, you couldn't find it? You weren't sure if they figured you were lying, or so dumb you just couldn't remember where it happened on your own body.

That sure doesn't happen on the car. You ding it and then try to figure out how to hide it. It just stays there. Three weeks later, it is still there. It's just going to be more obvious when the car gets washed.

Why can't somebody bottle whatever it is that makes our skin heal? We could run in the house, get the stuff and brush it on the car. A week later—hey, the dent is gone and the paint is back before anyone notices.

Face it; it's great how our skin heals. Bruises, cuts, scrapes, gashes, insect bites, poison oak, allergies, sunburn, punctures—we've had them all. What would we look like today if we had every wound, blemish and ailment our skin ever had ALL on us right now? Yuck, we'd look worse than lizard-faced zombies. And that's just looks. We would probably feel even worse than we look.

What if the ability of our skin to heal was bottled somehow? Wow! Little brother comes crying to mommy because he scraped his knee; his pants bloody and a hole in the knee. We thought the pants were ruined but not with the bottled stuff. Just brush it on, throw it in the hamper and by next week... you can't find the hole or stain.

We could pour it into our house paint and never have to paint again. It heals all flaws; great on furniture; great on tires. The tire treads are always deep. Carpet wearing out at home? It could be as thick and fluffy as the day you bought it.

To tell you the truth, I wish my teeth healed as well as my skin.

Come on you scientists, enough with the computers, make us a bottle.

OUR EYES, YET UNBORN

How many things that happen everyday, seem like miracles, but since they happen every day, we just ignore them?

The idea of a single, fertilized cell not only reproducing itself but reproducing every kind of cell needed in a human body is... well, mind-boggling. Even the literal creation of eyes from a single cell is a marvel. Consider the complexities: the veins within the eye, the iris and the muscles of the iris to contract and dilate the pupil, the lens, the cornea and incredibly, the ability to see. Both eyes are neatly seated in eye sockets, a cooperative setting with the skull. Tear ducts run to the eyes to keep them moist. Muscles attach to the eyes for efficient movement of the eyes. They're furnished with nerves for feeling and nerves for communication, all linked to the brain.

What struck me today, is reading about the eyelids' development when we were still little fetuses in our mother's belly. At three months after conception (six months before birth), the eyelids are tightly closed covering our eyes. When I say, "closed," I mean for you to understand that each eye is covered with a single thin sheet of skin. Yes, like some blind mole or alien creature, we all had our eyes securely protected with a solid lid while our eyes were forming. Almost magically, in the sixth month, an invisible "blade" precisely slices a clean crossways cut. It divides the single covering into two, exactly in half, providing the NEW ability to open and shut our eyelids. How does that happen?

Of course, the muscles to open and shut our eyelids are also in place. There are three distinct operations of the eyelids: First, the *voluntary* movements to close our eyes, wink or shut out light. Second, to *involuntarily* blink our eyes to keep them wet. Third, is the *instinctive* reactionary response to blink when an object appears to threaten or damage the eye.

It is not until the sixth or seventh month that eyebrows and eyelashes appear while still in the womb.

Construction jobs require financing, time schedules, supervisors and workers of many skills to erect a building. With the millions of cells in each eye, a building is a primitive project in comparison. If there is controversy in your mind about that, consider how many buildings there are in the world built by men. Next, consider how many functioning *eyeballs* men have constructed. Zilch, none, zero eyeballs that can see. I know glass eyeballs are a big business, but oh how wonderful it would be if we could actually build seeing eyes for the blind.

Who sets the time schedules for the building of our eyes while we are still fetuses? It is the same schedule for all babies worldwide and for all generations.

Whose blueprint do all the supervisors follow so all these cells, muscles, nerves, hair, lens, cornea, iris, blood vessels, bones and skin work together?

Who trains the workers to construct such brilliant, technical equipment? Their skill exceeds the skill of the entire world's science that has yet to succeed in building such wondrous things as a single seeing eye?

There seems to be an entire array of various specialists just to construct our eyes during the pre-born stage of development. What incredible army constructed our entire body? Whew.

All accidents? Nah, I'm a little crazy, but not that crazy.

MULTI-TASKING EAR

As kids, we would walk around the house pretending to be blind. We would bump into things and all agree how hard it would be. It isn't as common to do that with our ears and practice being deaf. It is just another one of those amazing things that we take for granted.

How about that yucky ear wax? We have 2,000 special glands in each ear canal to manufacture that stuff. It's called "cerumen." It traps the dust, dirt, and those incredibly loud bugs that seem to love our ears so much. It's the new wax that does most of the cleaning. The new wax pushes out the old wax. We all want clean ears, but the new wax is good stuff that includes a chemical that helps kill germs.

There is a strange combination of functions in our ears. Not only can we distinguish over 1,500 musical tones (a piano has only 88 keys), but right there in middle of listening functions is the critical function of balance. Hey, not my invention. This balancing equipment is also pretty slick. You have three small curved tubes (semi-circular canals) that are all filled with fluid. Right there, where you will never shave, inside of those 3 curved tubes in your ears are microscopic hairs. These hairs are planted on a layer of jelly. Of course, this is for a reason. It's no accident. Any movement of your body makes that fluid move inside of all three of those 3 curved tubes. When the fluid moves, it bends those little tiny hairs and when those little tiny hairs move it sends a signal to your brain. You know how liquid stays level in a tilted glass. Same idea. High-tech stuff, huh?

Wait, it gets better. Those little tiny hairs have little tiny crystals *balancing, yes balancing,* on top of the hairs. Why, you ask? This gives your entire body a sense of which way is up and which way is down in relation to gravity (another interesting invention). For instance, when you tilt your head, the gravity causes the crystals to fall from their tiny perch atop the little tiny hairs. The slight movement of the crystals falling bends the hairs sending more signals to the brain so you know where up is.

We can't even tune up your balance with a crystal overhaul, let alone give you a new set of crystals, hairs and fresh jelly. So whadya think? Look at what we have here. We tie in the properties of gravity with a network of nerves to send information to the brain. And then we program the brain so it knows what to do with those signals. Some signals are for balancing. Other signals are for automatic instincts saving us from a fall. Still other signals are for detecting sounds like music or a sarcastic tone of voice.

Folks, there's nobody nowhere that can make anything like what you have already right inside of your ears. Now can you really listen to anyone tell you that your ears were made by accident?

Could You Invent An Ear?

Do you know Morse code? *Dot dot dot—dash dash dash—dot dot dot;* that's SOS, a signal for help.

In the late 1800's and early 1900's, people in the telegraph office would punch out codes for messages all across the country. The telegraph, using Morse code, was the "telephone" of its day.

For Morse code they would use their finger to tap out the message. Now imagine the top piece being tapped as a little hammer and underneath a little anvil.

Guess what? In your *middle ear* are two bones called the *hammer* and *anvil.* They tap out a code too. The vibration from sound vibrates the eardrum that shakes the hammer that hits the anvil that sends that information to your brain with every sound you hear. Do you know what is tapping out that code? It is the eardrum vibrating. Instead of hearing different levels of vibration, like the dots and dashes of Morse code, you hear SOUND. The brain TRANSLATES the code into sounds. Instead of just vibrations, thanks to your brain, you hear voices, music, motors, birds, the breeze, ocean waves, and all the sounds of life.

Before you could invent such a device (an ear) you would need to understand more about how sound works. You would need to know about sound waves and that those waves are vibrations of different frequencies. Ideally, what would be most sensitive to sound waves traveling through the air? Not a rock. Not dirt. Ideally, something thin and delicate like a stretched out balloon would translate the sound waves into visible vibrations that you could both see and feel.

Let me ask you, which simple life form or fish do you think originally came up with the idea of an ear, even a primitive ear? Of course, the idea of hearing and how to detect sounds could only be deduced after understanding some basic principles of audio waves and frequencies. A more sophisticated ear could only be designed after a greater understanding of acoustics, characteristics of sound waves. Then you would also need to know things such as sound wave properties, the speed of sound and the interaction of sound with matter and organisms. This is the easy part. After all that is figured out, we have to invent a code that translates all this to the brain so it is not just different speeds of vibrations humming. To finish the job we have to invent a new part of the brain to process this information. Finally, we also have to develop some communication system between the ear and the brain that connects these incredible inventions.

Maybe a simple life form couldn't devise all of this. Maybe it was an incredibly smart fish. Or, maybe it was a dumb fish with really smart DNA, but who designed the really smart DNA? Gee, maybe it was just really lucky that all these things fell into place for every living species on earth that can hear.

We *copied* the basic idea of making thin membranes in speakers and telephones but we are not anywhere near duplicating the fantastic coordinated design in the ear, human or animal. If we could duplicate it, there would be no deaf people in America. We have yet to even copycat the intelligence that looms beyond our reach even in designing an ear.

I hear music. I hear a baby laugh. I hear the wind blow and the coyotes howl. But not only can I hear these things, dogs and cats turn their heads to the same sounds I hear. How?

Understanding The Meaning Of Sounds

Many creatures throughout the earth have very similar designs equipping them to be able to detect sound. The design is so similar it is almost as though they are different versions, models and types from the same manufacturer.

What is even more interesting to me and that I have yet to hear addressed, is how did the animals get an *understanding* of sounds made by animals among their own species?

Mating calls are not only sounds heard by certain animals but also *understood* by that species. Where and how did species gain understanding as to what a specific sound means? To an untrained ear, it is just an animal or bird making noise.

A cat's hiss is not a friendly gesture by any cat. A rattlesnake's rattle is not a mating call. A coyote does not howl when confronting an enemy. So not only has the incredible invention of the ear AND sound been designed but also the instinctive and universal ability of species to interpret the meaning of certain sounds. This is unlike much of the human language where sounds do not always have universal meanings.

The sound "we" means "us" to Americans but "yes" *(oui)* to a Frenchmen.

"See" means "to look" in English but "yes"(*sí*) in Spanish.

Even in America "bad" meant "no good" fifteen years ago, but now "bad" means "cool" which used to mean "a low temperature" but now means "fashionable?" But who says "how fashionable" nowadays?

A cat's hiss or a bird's mating call means the same thing in California as New Jersey or Germany. A cat's hiss or a bird's mating call means the same thing today as it did in 2000 B.C.

If I get a male cat from China, France or Sudan and bring it to California and it meets another male cat that hisses at it, they both know it is not a friendly greeting.

Wolves and coyotes howl. Dolphins and whales have a language.

I must therefore conclude that science needs to answer multiple questions; first,

1. Before designing a component that can detect sound, don't we first need to understand the properties of sound?
2. Who or what was smart enough to successfully design an ear when it was first invented?
3. For an ear to hear sound, doesn't it need to be connected to a brain?

But shouldn't we also address the uncanny ability of entire species to universally agree on the meaning of certain sounds?

There are no homonyms in the animal kingdom. A homonym is a word that sounds the same as another word but has different meaning. Like, "threw" and "through" or "knead" and "need." Along the same line is, one word with different meanings like "cast" as in "to cast a fishing line," "the cast of a play" or "broken arm in a cast."

The exact same sound having different meanings just doesn't exist in the animal kingdom. Yet creatures of the same species communicate without having agreed on the meanings of sounds.

This improbable feature that is so vast and extraordinary demands that at least the question be asked by the scientific community.

If all the greatest scientific minds can't answer these questions now, who or what put it together when it was invented, something without brains, a roll of the dice or somebody smart?

You have a brain pick your favorite from those three.

MUSCLE CARS

A professor in Australia, Uwe Proske, published his findings regarding muscles. He was intrigued with the observation that unfamiliar movements, such as running backwards, caused aches the day after for both athletes and couch potatoes.

This can be temporary even when the exercise is frequent. Here's how it works:

All of our muscle fibers are made up of two basic proteins; sounds simple so far.

Those two simple proteins are organized into millions of regimented units the educated call "sarcomeres." These sarcomeres can expand, which is important for muscles. However, when pushed to the limit they *snap*. Ouch! Now we have broken sarcomeres. When enough sarcomeres are broken, muscle fibers actually die, according to the report. When our body has trouble and we don't know what to do, it is amazing how the body DOES know what to do. It is wisdom beyond sophisticated technology again. Not surprisingly, our body sends help in the form of repair enzymes. Call it the built-in medical team, if you want. It's those repair enzymes that cause the soreness you feel the day after. The news gets better. The body's repair enzymes not only replace the old broken muscle fiber with new muscle fiber but this new fiber is always stronger than the previous. Instead of simply repairing what is broken, it improves it. This is done by providing more sarcomeres per muscle fiber, decreasing the chance of future breakage (and soreness).

Remember "muscle cars"? They are older cars with big engines. But how would you like real muscles on cars? How much would the "Muscle Option" cost? Normally, if you drive your car in the mountains, the winding roads put extra strain on the shocks and springs. This will cause extra wear and higher repair bills.

Our fantasy of having the "Muscle Option" works differently, like our own muscles. If you live in the mountains, that extra strain begins rebuilding a stronger frame, stronger springs and stronger shocks after the strain while it is resting and parked. After a few weeks, your car is handling the road better than ever.

Are those sharp turns wearing out your tires early? Get the "Muscle Option." Extra stress on the treads activates the "Muscle Option" and the durability of the tires *increase*, especially where the wearing is greatest. In a week, you notice your treads are deeper, the tires are now thicker and your car is in better shape because of the strain.

Yeah, don't we wish? Sounds like technology way beyond our own, and it is. You think the guy that could invent the "Muscle Option" would become a millionaire?

Our minds and bodies are best preserved with use, not pampering.

More mileage on a car decreases its value. More wear weakens it. Our own human bodies are designed differently. More physical stress creates strength and endurance.

We seem to improve with challenges. It's the way we were designed.

In The Kitchen
Alibrando's Ripple 2 of Law #9
Deduced Intention

This is a ripple of Law #9 relating intelligence to order. If Law #9 is true about order and intelligence being related, and the 1st ripple concludes the unlikelihood of order coming from accidents then here is a 3rd ripple: Design is intentional. If it is no accident then, of course, it is on purpose.

Un-provable Notion: Just because there is intelligent design, millions of flourishing species and an untold number of systems coordinated into a seamless, interdependent system doesn't mean it was done on purpose.

Sensible Fact: If a complex invention works, it was probably made to do it on purpose.

TECHNICAL WORDING: *The likelihood of conscious, intelligent intention increases exponentially with an increase in order.*

Below, the graphic represents progressions that are equal.

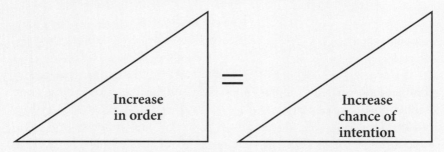

Now, let's do something a little different. Take 5 marbles and set them down in a straight row. If you tried that 10 times, how many times do you think you could succeed? 10 out of 10, I'd say.

What about 20 marbles? Line those up in a row. You could even go one-step further and not only line them up in a row, but also space them apart so that they are equally spaced and in a straight in a row. How many times out of 10 attempts can you line up 20 marbles successfully? I'd say 10 out of 10 with some effort.

Take the same 20 marbles and keep throwing them up in the air until they land in a straight row equally spaced. Maybe you won't live long enough to see that happen, although it is theoretically possible.

There is something to observe here. With intelligent effort, simple design is easy but this is not true without intelligent involvement.

This proves the decreasing likelihood of *order by accident* in contrast to *order from conscious, intelligent intention.*

Also, the gap between conscious, intelligent intention and random accident widens with greater order. It is very easy with intelligence to line up a row of 50 marbles but almost impossible for it to happen accidentally.

The gap widens not in proportion to the order but more dramatically. It is not additional or even just multiplication, but *exponential* multiplication.

Anyone wanting to dispute the actual numbers is welcome to do so, but I promise the pattern and exponential proportions will be similar to what is displayed here.

Marbles in a Straight Row

marbles	random	intentional
2	1:1	1:1
3	1:40	1:1
4	1:150	1:1
5	1:1000	1:1
10	1:40000	1:1

Somebody somewhere has probably already done this experiment. That is what science is, experiments and conclusions, not theories and philosophies without experiments.

We are talking about marbles in a row as an example of order and look at the numbers showing the possibility of accidental order. We are not talking about the order in a car or house. A car or house, because it is so much more organized than a row of marbles, having the chance of accidentally being built becomes ridiculous. The idea of intention follows. To end up with enough order and function as found in a house with electricity, plumbing, roofing, lights, etc. is far more likely to be on purpose—intentional, than accidental. Don't you agree?

Taking it up another notch… if we compare a house or car to the sophistication of even one eyeball, the house or car is simple and primitive in comparison. So much so that man can build a car or house but not a seeing eyeball.

To say a functioning, seeing eyeball successfully connected to the brain while fitting perfectly in an eye socket with watering properties, instinctive eyelids for protection with eyelashes and coordination between two eyes to see things in three dimensions requires intelligence is an understatement. To omit the point that it was made on purpose to function so well is downright criminal against all logic and science.

I say what I am describing is in fact provable scientific law. This is a vivid example of:

RIPPLE 2 OF LAW #9
The likelihood of conscious, intelligent intention increases exponentially with an increase in order.

RELATED ARTICLES:
Stonehenge versus the Universe

SLEEPING ON THE JOB

Like you and me the scientists have observed many things, but there is so much more we do not understand.

Sleep is more than recovery from energy that has been drained. It is not just a "re-charge." The discovery has been made, through research on mice, that sleep is essential to life. Sleep is not essential to simple life forms but critical to higher life forms.

This whole subject gets quite involved but I encourage you to appreciate all the unknown benefits your body, your emotions and your brain get from sleep.

Often I am thankful for the end of a rough day. Going to sleep is sort of closing the chapter. I usually wake up renewed and more willing to face another day rather than prolonging the last day. If we didn't have to sleep, I think we would miss it.

According to encyclopedias and other books on the subject, sleep is observed ONLY in humans and animals that have *highly developed nervous systems*. Did you catch that? "Highly developed nervous systems" only! Not all animals have them. Even creatures as complicated as reptiles, remain scientifically controversial as to whether or not they really sleep. Some animals exhibit resting periods, BUT NOT SLEEP. It's a science thing (rest isn't sleep).

Birds and mammals, including humans, don't just shut down during sleep. Our nervous system literally shifts into modes that are different from wakefulness, but that are not necessarily less active. In other words, the nervous system is not necessarily less active but simply doing something very different during sleep. Your nervous system is busy doing things in you and for you while you are unconscious.

None of us knows much about sleep because when we experience it we are sort of not here—unconscious. We are aware that we dream. We have memories about how we felt before and after sleep. We even know how we feel after being disturbed out of our sleep. But what can we say about what is actually happening to us *while* we sleep?

As a kid, I used to try to see what happened to me when I went to sleep. The next morning I'd be bummed out because I kept missing it. I'd try again and again and from personal experience I'll tell you, I never did get to see myself fall asleep.

How I love sleep. Trees don't sleep. Rocks don't sleep. The water doesn't sleep. Cells don't sleep (sheep sleep).

How does one design such a thing as sleep and dreams, and develop them so that they work? Think about this. How do you invent sleep? First, it must be an idea. When you think about trying to figure this out, it is mind-boggling.

How do you invent a different type of consciousness for sleeping? It's been invented.

How do you cause something like dreaming to evolve when you sleep, when it didn't exist anywhere? Who slipped the idea of dreaming into the human experience? It is here and it is very important to both our physical and emotional health.

We take so many things for granted. Despite our ignorance about sleep, we are not prevented from benefiting from it. If you can't take a nice nap today, go to bed fifteen minutes early tonight just to enjoy the whole idea that you get to sleep while your body does all kinds of work for you. Sleep tight.

CAN'T BE ALL HEART OR ALL BRAIN

I had the privilege of receiving training to become a "First Responder" as a Big Creek Volunteer Firefighter. The critical ABC's of emergency care is Airway, Breathing, and Circulation. These are critical areas that, if not working, could quickly kill a person while waiting for an ambulance.

We all feel so immortal, since none of us remembers being NON-existent. Yet, a few minutes without oxygen can kill us or permanently damage us for the rest of our mortal life.

Teachers emphasized how the blood brings the vital oxygen to the brain. Did you make sure oxygenated blood was constantly flowing to your brain today? It keeps you alive.

The entire world's medical profession knows that blood must get to the brain and that oxygen must get to the blood via the lungs so that blood can carry that oxygen to the brain.

It doesn't matter what nation you live in, this is still true. It doesn't matter what age the patient is; they will certainly die without blood carrying oxygen to the brain. It doesn't matter what the doctor's philosophy or religion is; the oxygenated blood must continually reach the brain or the patient dies.

Philosophy and language take a back seat to the unyielding truth of this simple, critical fact. This is an absolute.

Many philosophers say there are no absolutes, but the blood is absolutely pumping oxygen to their brain when they say that.

Here is design, consistent throughout all humanity. Doctors don't challenge it. Chemists don't question it. Evolutionists don't deny it. Religious people die without it, hypocrites and saints alike. Good people, bad people, all people need the oxygenated blood to their brain.

Who decided this irrefutable necessity? Who designed this blood-pumping organ, the carefully organized blood with plasma, white blood cells to fight uninvited germs, clotting ability and so much more? Who designed the incredible brain that manages the support of our body without our conscious wisdom?

Science has given environmentalists the ammunition to protect nature around us since the interdependence of all nature is so vast and deep and still being learned. Likewise, in our own bodies, we are so interlinked. It's not just a heart that we need; the heart is doing a vital job. But like the ABC's of medical emergency, although the patient's heart is beating if he is not breathing, he will still die because the blood going to his brain lacks the oxygen.

We need the heart. We need the brain. We need the lungs. Our internal organs and systems are very interdependent, like nature is very interdependent. But we are also vitally interlinked with our environment. That vital oxygen is in the air we breathe. That oxygen which is a waste product of all vegetation is life to us. To live, we need the oxygen that is protected from the winds of space by the veil of our ozone layer. It is a world in which we thrive. This is all so incredibly woven together with such beauty and harmony. The ingenuity exceeds all comprehension, not slightly, but overwhelmingly.

We must admit not only is there much more that we don't know, we have no idea and no way to measure how much we do not know.

IN THE KITCHEN
Alibrando's Ripple 3 of Law #9
Functional Design

Rippling outward, if order is related to intelligence and 1) it is no accident and 2) it is done on purpose then 3) working technology is certainly proof of intelligence.

UN-PROVABLE NOTION: Brilliant engineering does not require intelligence.

SENSIBLE FACT: Working order is always evidence of intelligence.

TECHNICAL WORDING: *Any functioning technology is proof of intelligence.*

Below, the graphic represents that when one exists, so does the other, without exception.

| Working Technology | = | Proof of Intelligence |

The opposite way of stating the same truth would be:

| Working Technology ≠ Accidental Mistake |

EXPLAINING THE LAW

Art can be order but it is not technology. Straight lines and geometric design can display order. Symmetry and other things can be coordinated to show order. However, technology is design with functional purpose. It is a design that actually *does something*. The *appearance* of order is secondary to the fact that it functions. To design technology requires intelligence, thinking and calculating. It is result-oriented thinking.

Technology is certainly not an ongoing series of random accidents creating ingenious inventions.

Highly trained doctors and scientists fervently work to unravel the secrets of various technologies in the human body. With all of today's modern technology, the technologies working just in the human body far exceed the achievements of science so far. To make a quadriplegic well, a deaf person hear, a blind person see—would be called a miracle by today's standards. Presently we are helplessly baffled although impressed by the intricate complexities of so many interdependent systems that together make these "technologies" work in our bodies.

A bow and arrow is technology also. A piece of rock tied to a wooden handle with leather straps is technology. These technologies enable its user to perform tasks better than without these functioning tools.

Invention and technology are conspicuously NOT a sign of unintelligence or lack of intelligence. It would be irrational to assume that functional technology is a sign of random error. By definition, random occurrence is NOT the application of anything, but instead a mere accident.

Most often we observe random accidents ruining things, not fixing them; a tree branch dropping on a car, the wind blowing dirt on a newly painted fence or lightning causing a fire. Even tripping on a rock and breaking your wrist, crashing into a wall, spilling grape juice and staining the carpet are examples of the bad results of accidents.

It is normal to conclude problems or things breaking down as the result of random error. What rational person considers random accidents causing solutions instead of problems? Therefore, I would propose:

RIPPLE 3 OF LAW #9
Any functioning technology is proof of intelligence.

RELATED ARTICLES:
Stonehenge versus the Universe
Science Keeps Proving How Little We Know

OUR OWN TOXIC DEFENSE
In prosperous America, the quantity of pollutants we inhale is tiny compared to all the toxins we cram down our throats. Most poisons entering our body are from happily buying junk food with our hard-earned money and eating it. We bombard our body with an untold number of unhealthy chemicals, including preservatives, caffeine, alcohol, and even sugar. We need a seriously brilliant plan and a small army of defenders to save our lives from our own eating habits.

Such things do exist! Our own liver is one part of the ingenious plan. One of the liver's main jobs is to neutralize toxins and poisons. Once neutralized, the toxins (now harmless waste) are "shipped" out through the bloodstream or out through the bladder.

Not only do we overdose the poor liver with all sorts of dangerous chemicals; we starve it while not feeding ourselves necessary nutrients. To do battle for us, our liver and entire body craves nourishment. Like us, our body weakens when deprived of necessary fuel.

With incredible foresight, there is a Plan B that can be set in motion if the liver has too much work and not enough energy. If there is still trouble, there is even a Plan C

When the liver "realizes" it can no longer handle all the toxins we give to it, it finally gives up on neutralizing the toxins and simply imprisons them. This is Plan B, holding the toxins captive in the liver. That is the best an overworked liver can do to protect your blood and body from those threatening toxins. Neutralizing them altogether is Plan A. But if denied proper nourishment; Plan B is still saving you. Instead of just poisoning your whole blood system and body, Plan B saves you as well as Plan A, but at greater sacrifice and risk.

Do we care? Not usually. We keep eating the junk and skip the fresh fruits and vegetables. Still the poisons and toxins keep coming and eventually our faithful liver has to go to Plan C. Plan C is a call for help. The liver is not the only organ willing to sacrifice itself to save us. A cooperative effort goes into motion in response to the liver's plea. The liver "asks the cells" to take some toxic overload. The request is that the cells begin taking some toxins hostage too. Cells do not have the equipment to neutralize toxins as the liver does. The priority is to keep the blood pure. The cells agree, now taking as many toxins prisoner as they can hold.

Do we care? Not usually, unless we get sick.

Often, what we call sickness is our body trying to save us.

All the while, the body itself kicks in multiple ways of getting rid of poisons. "Going to the bathroom" is the regular ongoing process. Diarrhea is a quicker remedy. Sweating is another. A fever can literally burn up some toxins. Ulcers can release more toxins through a hole. Sneezes and a runny nose can also rid the body of more toxins.

Completely losing your appetite during illness can temporarily force you to fast. This diverts huge amounts of energy away from digestion and focuses limited resources to fighting toxins and cleansing your body.

Do we care? Naturally, we want to immediately get rid of the symptoms instead of letting our defense network do its work. We take medicine to stop diarrhea, to lower our fever, to plug up the ulcers, and to stop our runny noses. We just want to feel good so we can go back to eating all that junk again, like we are used to doing.

What can happen if the toxins vastly outnumber the defenses in our body? Helpful cells that are holding toxins prisoner can accidentally become toxic and start reproducing themselves in that toxic state. It is like a rebellion when your own body that has valiantly been protecting you begins reproducing threats to your own body.

This is not advice about eating or medicine. It is rather an appreciative look at a small part of a remarkable network. Look at the spectacular strategic defense in each of our own bodies. It is incredible how much wiser our bodies seem to be than we are ourselves.

What is the real source of such detailed thinking that could plan systems like this? What mind can conceive and design defenders within our body that almost seem to think for themselves, even when we operate against our own health?

If we cannot understand it—if we cannot duplicate it—at least we can admire it.

In The Kitchen
Alibrando's Ripple 4 of Law #9
Proportional Intelligence

The final ripple in this book of Law #9, if order is related to intelligence and 1) it is no accident and 2) it is done on purpose then 3) working technology is proof of intelligence and 4) the greater the design, the smarter the designer.

The emphasis here is the obvious conclusion or ripple effect of agreeing with the others.

Un-provable Notion: The complexity of technology has no relation to intelligence.

Sensible Fact: The more complex an invention is, the smarter the inventor.

Technical Wording: *In proportion to the sophistication of the design, is the sophistication of the designer's intelligence.*

Below, the graphic represents relative progressions.

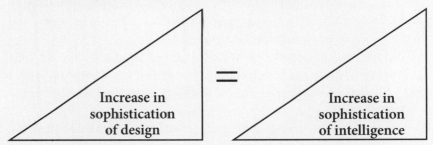

Explaining the Law

If we are stranded on an island together and while exploring we discover a circle of rocks with ashes in the middle, what are we are going to think?

If I said, "Wow, what are the odds of this happening by accident?" you would think I was nuts.

What we would do is this: We would look at one another and wonder "WHO made this fire?"

Consider the meaning of you agreeing with what I just said. A simple circle of rocks around ashes would clearly lead us to believe someone, too intelligent to be animal, made the fire in a circle of rocks to keep the fire within that circle.

At this point, we cannot determine the degree of intelligence, but clearly, it is proof of intelligence.

We continue exploring the island and discover a home. It is not a hut or primitive tent, but a structure with a shingled roof made of island materials. We are impressed with the slight elevation above the ground and well-made steps. We approach the door and knock. With no response, we notice the door is hung on a horizontal pole with a type of twine. It is a sliding door. We enter and find chairs, a table and a soft bed, all made from island materials. We are impressed with this person's skill and conclude it is not some primitive native, but someone as smart as or maybe smarter than us.

We leave and the next day continue exploring and encounter something strange. It is a metallic, oblong contraption about 14 feet long and maybe 6 feet wide. It has what appears to be a shiny, dark covering on top. It doesn't look broken at all and appears very advanced. We look at each other in amazement.

We continue touching and it has buttons. One of the buttons makes a beeping sound and the shiny dark covering suddenly becomes transparent. Through the now transparent top we can see two seats inside and what appears to be something like a cockpit.

We drop our jaws and look at each other in astonishment. We have never seen anything like this and I say, "I hope this guy is human" with a grin, "because whoever made this is definitely smarter than both of us."

End of story.

Observation: We recognized intelligence with the circled ashes. We acknowledged greater intelligence when we found the well-built dwelling. After we saw the advanced craft, we were impressed with intelligence greater than our own.

Although any design reveals intelligence, more complex design reveals greater intelligence. Therefore, I propose:

Ripple 4 of Law #9

In proportion to the sophistication of the design, is the sophistication of the designer's intelligence.

Below, is another graphic related to our island story representing that the designer's intelligence is proportional to the sophistication of that object's design.

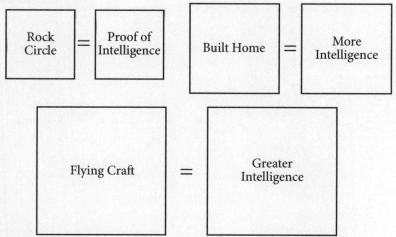

RELATED ARTICLES:
Imitation is the Highest Form of Flattery
The Three Little Pigs

Pleasure

Enjoyment… satisfaction… gratification… these are pleasures my lawn mower will never experience, no matter how expensive the mower is.

Pleasure, what a concept! What an idea!

Your tongue can detect that which is bitter, sweet, sour and if food has gone bad. That is important to survival. But to eat something nutritious that is also satisfying to the tongue creates pleasure. It feels good. I know I enjoy dinner much more than my car enjoys a gas fill-up.

The huge junk food and candy markets have tapped into the pleasure zone of the tongue, usually without nutrition and often to the injury of the body. The ability to experience pleasure has led to addictions and disorders in abundance. Is pleasure bad? Of course not! It is the cherry on top. We not only live, but experience pleasure in multiple realms.

Which of man's inventions experience their own pleasure? Jets, trains, atomic submarines, appliances, solar powered satellites… you name it, none experience pleasure.

How hard would it be to give the ability to experience pleasure to any of our manufactured products? Sure, I suppose we could program a computer to make sounds of satisfaction when we did certain things. However, this is not the computer genuinely feeling good or feeling pleasure. It would be a sound that we humans related to pleasure. Hearing that sound would please us, not the computer.

Why would science or manufacturers even go to the trouble or expense to attempt such a venture as creating the sense of pleasure? It serves no purpose. It creates no profit. Genuine pleasure would only be felt by the object, not the manufacturer or customer. In the realm of efficiency, productivity, and survival, *pleasure* is extra baggage. I doubt if it is even within the power of science to grasp the concept of manufacturing the ability to experience pleasure, but I have a bigger question. If it is extra baggage, and serves no critical purpose, what would prompt its invention in evolution?

What DNA, what simple life form, what element, what micro-organism could possibly have come up with the idea of pleasure before it even existed as a concept? Does DNA, alone, have the intelligence and initiative to create and design the ability for an organism to experience pleasure? And the bigger question… why? What possible purpose could it serve other than the pleasure it would give the designer to see the product experience pleasure?

If you give someone a back massage, it is for his/her pleasure. If the person giving the massage is experiencing pleasure they are either unselfish or care so much for the recipient that they enjoy making them happy.

Then what kind of inventor would invent pleasure for his invention?

Here is my theory. Whoever invented pleasure already had that ability. That ability to feel pleasure was then designed and put into the experience of humans and other creatures because the idea pleased the designer.

Got a better theory?

YEAH, WHAT ABOUT THAT?

FROM ONE HEAD TO ANOTHER

As you glance down at the black markings on this page, you are distinguishing them as symbols (letters). To a person who cannot read, they are meaningless marks.

These marks form words, depending on how they are grouped together. Very quickly, your eyes are scanning these symbols. Rapidly, you continue deciphering each letter grouping into the word it represents. Without realizing how quickly you are doing this, you are also assembling the sequence of these words forming meaningful communication called a sentence. Without hesitation, you continue decoding these marks at such a rapid rate that the marks become a virtual "voice" speaking to you. The "voice" is the expression of the writer's thoughts conveyed to your eyes and almost instantly to your mind. As these thoughts are conveyed via writing, your own mind not only interprets the words and sentences but at the same time is analyzing *the meaning* of the thoughts and comparing it to your own thoughts and ideas.

You do not need to stop reading and then think about what you read. You are still reading, interpreting and analyzing at the same time and also accepting or rejecting all or part of what is being communicated. Incredibly, added to all of this lightning speed thought and interaction between the marks on this page and your own mind, your personality responds emotionally as well, by the millisecond, to every new idea expressed. You agree and it may feel good or even great, depending on your own ideas, values and personality. You may disagree and be bored, agitated, angry or frustrated.

It is incredible, the power of thought.

I think my own thoughts. A portion of them I can try to describe in what is called "written language." I can write or type my thoughts on paper. If I choose, I can send them to a newspaper, magazine or book publisher who in turn distributes this written language in their publication. Then, you turn the page and look at those same marks and now, my thoughts are entering your brain. Think about it. Even after I die, using these same marks or written language, my thoughts can enter the minds of others.

Have you ever considered how absolutely amazing that is? It's almost creepy. Have you ever considered the phenomenal quantity of other people's thoughts you process every day through just reading?

What about TV? People write ideas for TV commercials. Others get the models, actors, artwork and props for the commercial. Still more people add sound effects and music. The script is delivered over air waves or cable in its final form to your TV; into your eyes, ears and brain. Your brain processes this information and the person that originally had an idea for a commercial has put his idea into your mind. You don't even know who he is, but he's put some of his ideas in your head.

You may now be thinking about commercials but actually, you are still scanning marks on a page. While reading, your own mind's memory may have pictured or remembered TV commercials you have seen—all this while you still continue to read.

I think we owe our brains some kind of standing ovation. Even if you don't think you're very smart, you really do have a powerful, almost unbelievably smart brain.

Now, last question, where did you get it?

IF WE EVOLVE, WHY CAN'T CARS?
Putting aside all evidence, or lack of evidence, of evolution, let me ask you some deeper questions. The evolutionary theory describes a process where, over billions of years, simple things become improved and more complex. It theorizes that something continually invents brand new species that did not previously exist. The whole of the evolutionary theory describes all things as having a "need" to improve.

Where does this "need" come from? Where does a simple one-celled organism get the quality of biological engineering genius to design and manufacture a better organism?

The kind of intelligence necessary exceeds all human intelligence today, and according to the theory, we humans are at the top of the evolution pyramid. What's wrong here?

The evolution theory contains unproven theories inside unproven theories. This theory itself has brand new ideas with no scientific soundness.

I will try to give a name to one of these strange ideas but first, let me describe it.

It is something physical that we cannot touch or analyze under a microscope. It supposedly lurks in everything that exists, having both the motivation and intelligence to improve the species or thing. In the evolutionary theory, it exists in every plant, every tree, every rock, every person, every star, every fish, bird, bug and chemical.

Let's call it the "IEP," standing for INVISIBLE EVOLUTIONARY POWER. This indwelt dynamic contained in all things maintains its focus to improve stuff and species over billions of years. It designs brand new species and then fashions a reproductive system.

Within each new species, the IEP constantly invents new ways to survive, and create more intelligence while originating completely new designs for eating, hunting, engineering and more.

According to evolutionary theory, somewhere… one day, the right chemicals come together under the right circumstances and BAM! The very first simple life form started looking for food.

Is it the IEP that also brought the right conditions together? Did the IEP have food right there handy next to the first living organism and a digestive system that could metabolize that food that was close by? And did the same IEP also give the first living organism the first invention of INSTINCT so that it instinctively knew to ingest that food that conveniently placed itself close by? The questions continue. Unfortunately, scientists have yet to re-create the transition of non-living to living even in a controlled environment.

If scientists cannot do it, we can conclude the IEP is smarter than all of humanity's greatest minds put together.

If this amazing IEP lingers in all things, would not a car left in a garage for years eventually develop at least a few improvements? Well, maybe thousands or millions of years would help. How about if you left your car in a garage for a billion years? Do you think it might improve its gas mileage or originate a totally new type of fuel system?

If this IEP idea seems a little ridiculous to you, that is a good sign that you are rational. On the other hand, if the Invisible Evolutionary Power idea sounds logical to you, possibly your respect for experts is greater than your confidence in your own thinking.

Personally, when I see intelligent design, I suspect intelligence with a purpose.

HOW WE INVENTED EXPERTS

What really makes a person an expert?

Some simply proclaim themselves experts. Others hold up papers saying they graduated from college or other training mediums and are now "experts." Still others become "experts" once they are paid for giving advice or a speech on a topic.

There is a whole cloud of confusion around the idea of expertise. When I was younger, I would read to find the "facts." Now I know I can find "experts" to back up *anything* I say is true.

That's a little scary, huh?

The experts are supposed to be the ones who tell us the "real truth" about science, psychology, religion or the economy. Nevertheless, in fact, they always disagree about something.

Serious "non-expert" seekers of truth, like me, might investigate the very information the "experts" were looking at to draw their "expert" conclusions.

Oh no. I would often find their research based on the conclusions of other "experts." So what is true? Such is the case in dating old bones and extinct animals.

Carbon-14 dating is by far the most extensively used method. This is how we "know" these skeletons were "1 million years old" or "20 million years old."

I will not get too seriously technical here so let me tell you something right up front ... they tested a LIVING mollusk (a mollusk is a shelled animal like a snail or a clam) with carbon dating, and by that dating method it was supposedly thousands of years old.

It's not exactly a foolproof or dependable method. As a matter of fact, it's kind of like drawing a compass on paper to get out of the woods.

It was surprising to me to discover there are at least five different kinds of dating methods. With the exception of Dendrochronology (counting tree rings), three are very rough and inconsistent. The popular one, Radiometric or Radiocarbon (C-14) dating, is based on THEORY!

Remember that a theory is NOT a fact, but an unproved guess.

You cannot send a man to jail based on theory instead of evidence. Conviction requires evidence. However, in science we permit misleading millions of people with unproved theories, without evidence, posing as science.

Under the theory of radiometric dating, there are six methods. However, note, they are ALL BASED ON THEORY.

The theory includes a "half-life" calculation. Half, based on what? Well, that's another guess. Remember, we are trying to determine age, so how do we know what half of that undetermined age is? The more I explain, the more confusing it will get. You can get answers to my questions but you won't understand it. When you study it more and more and eventually get to the bottom of it, you will find it is in fact a theory. Ultimately, there are expert opinions, certain assumptions and more guessing, although honest scientific effort is exerted.

When they want to measure how close they were to the right number of years, they will often cross-check the method on trees. That's because we know the tree dating method is scientific and dependable. When they carbon date something else they are postulating, based on what was pretty close on the tree, that it will be as accurate on other materials. Translation: they are still guessing.

There is a newer method of dating now called "High Speed Dating." When analyzing seeds from an Egyptian site estimated by archaeologists to be 20,000 years old, the new system dated the same seeds to be 200 years old. Is this method 100% accurate? Not yet, but it may be better than other methods. I honestly can't tell you, but it underscores my point: There really is disagreement about many things in the scientific community, especially things that cannot be proven with certainty.

This is not an article on Carbon dating but rather on how we often assume experts' assumptions are facts and not assumptions. This is a big mistake!

Check the facts and mentally put *theories* in a different place. You can build with facts; building with theories might be building a house of straw. Just know the difference mentally.

I notice many of the theories that remain unchallenged are ones with BIG words or ideas that go over our heads.

As we realize we cannot follow what they are saying, we simply wait for the bottom line. For example, consider the following conversation:

"So, what are you saying?"

"We know the world is approximately 15 million years old based on dating methods discovered by scientists who, using scientific properties, can determine ages."

"How do you get that number?"

"Well, one favorite method is measuring the carbon in a sample by counting the pulses of radiation emitted as each atom decays compared to, shall we say coal."

"Oh, Okay."

Of course we did not really understand—we just heard the word "scientists," "discovered," "determined" and some fancy science talk, so we trust that those guys must know what they're doing.

When we research, that usually means we find out what the experts say is true and our research is done. We need to just go one step further; we need to check THEIR research.

Experts are not another race of people. They were kids; they went to school just like us. Most of them watch TV just like us and then they do research, just like we could if that was our job.

That is exactly how we buy into so many ridiculous theories that are as un-scientific as the earth being flat. By the way, the earth being flat was once a long-standing *scientific* theory.

I remember asking questions about the Nebraska man and how science concluded entire sub-species of prehistoric humans existed for millions of years with the only evidence being one tooth.

All evidence has disappeared for the Peking man in China (Homo erectus). My college classmates at Camden County Community College, in New Jersey, would scoff telling me how ridiculous my questions were, but I was fortunate enough to have an honest science teacher who researched things himself. Although he did not agree with all my ideas, he would correct the class telling them that I made a good point and that there really was very little physical evidence of actual prehistoric man. It did not make me very popular with the rest of the class, however.

Expert opinions are still just opinions. If people are telling you that you are too stupid to understand what they understand, it doesn't mean what they claim is truly a fact.

I encourage you to challenge anything that does not line up with what you can personally understand. True understanding is rewarding.

Of course, an "expert" needs to know more than you do to be an expert. Naturally, if one expert knows much more than someone else, he may consider them inferior. But then again, that's just their expert opinion.

An expert opinion is an opinion, which in the opinion of other experts, is expert.

True science is almost the opposite of opinions. True science starts with a theory, conducts experiments to test that theory and then makes conclusions based on results, not opinions. True science does not bypass results and say, "We can't prove it but we still believe it." So the next time someone tells you that you don't know what you're talking about because "all the experts" say different, tell them why, in your own expert opinion, you disagree.

IN THE KITCHEN
Alibrando's Ripple 2 of Law #10
Consensus Myth

Using the ripple idea of certain conclusions leading to other conclusions, we have already figured out that an expert opinion is not the same as a fact. Certainly, certificates or degrees will never prevent any person holding those papers or endorsements from making mistakes.

Now we put a bunch of experts together and must reach the same conclusion: A bunch of expert opinions still don't make a FACT and mistakes are always possible.

UN-PROVABLE NOTION: Proof is required from amateurs but not necessarily from a group of experts.

SENSIBLE FACT: Expert guesses, beliefs, opinions (whether 1 or 1,000) are still not facts unless proven.

TECHNICAL WORDING: *Multiple expert opinions represent consensus, not fact.*

Certainly evidence is not wrong just because many experts agree it is wrong. And if there is no evidence to prove what many experts agree to be true, are we to believe them instead of evidence? Is it true that experts don't necessarily need to prove they are right?

> Collective opinion x 100 ≠ Fact

EXPLAINING THE LAW
There are fallacies in arguments. Some tricky tactics are so common they are listed as rules in formal debating. One false form of argument is called the "bandwagon" tactic. The idea, successfully used in advertising is "Everyone believes it so it must be true." This is a false basis for an argument but hugely influential. A majority of opinions still does not create a fact. Even if everyone on the planet believes the world is flat, it never changes the world's real shape.

Example 1: There is a joke about an insecure Indian Medicine Man who was supposed to predict the winter for his tribe through the old spiritual tradition of dancing and smoke. He told them that there would be plenty of snow this winter. Cautiously, he told the tribe that the spirits can change their mind. He would then secretly call the local weather bureau to get forecasts for the winter and ask about the upcoming winter. They would tell him there was going to be plenty of snow. Reassured, he would do the dance again with the "plenty of snow" forecast. Still insecure, he would regularly call the weather bureau to make sure there were no changes.

On one phone call he asked the weather bureau, "How do you guys figure this stuff out?"

"Well, we could check the Farmers' Almanac but we have more confidence in the local Indian Medicine Man, and he says there will plenty of snow this winter."

This really happens between some of our fields of science. They may base their expert opinion on another expert opinion. It is a comedy if one scientist bases his conclusions on two others that he wrongly supposes are absolutely correct.

We may have an accidental conspiracy.

Once reputations are at stake, however, the accidental conspiracy can become an intentional conspiracy. Nobody wants to be wrong.

This is a form of bandwagon logic. "If we all agree on what is true, it becomes true." The world is flat—anyone who disagrees shall be burned at the stake.

Reader, you must understand, this is invalid logic.

Scientific experts agreeing with each other does not equal scientific fact, whether accidental or intentional. Anything, if based on opinion rather than evidence, is not fact.

The solution is very simple. Provide evidence, not quotations. So I repeat:

Ripple 2 of Law #10
Multiple expert opinions represent consensus, not fact.

RELATED ARTICLES:
How We Invented Experts

WHAT OVERPOPULATION?

In the 60's and 70's, I heard and believed our world was overpopulated and the situation was worsening. I saw fields vanish and shopping centers appear. I saw traffic thicken. I saw science fiction movies frighten me with a world overcrowded, short of food, short of privacy and no space anywhere.

Sometime in the mid 70's I read a book called *Handbook on Population* by Robert L. Sassone. Boy, did I feel dumb. I then realized how easily I had been persuaded without ever questioning.

For instance, mathematically I could have calculated how much space people really have in the U.S. simply by dividing the population by square acres. The U.S. acreage totals about 2,270,000,000 square acres. A population of 225 million gives every single person more than 10 acres.

You can actually calculate these things for yourself. That's what was so embarrassing for me. I have flown across the country at night and for long periods seen only blackness below; then a treat, a city with lights. I would lean on my window gazing at the pretty lights of civilization and in less than a minute it was out of sight and the boring blackness returned. The obvious should have occurred to me then. There is more wilderness than civilization in America, even today.

Most people live in and around cities. That means most people live where they see crowded conditions becoming worse.

Cities all over the world are growing but the actual open space available is almost unbelievable.

Excluding Antarctica, the earth's landmass is about 52.5 million square miles. Now do you have any idea how many square miles are taken up by housing worldwide? According to UN statistics on housing from 1970, it was 9,000 square miles. I know these are old stats but I'll make up for it. The world population hasn't doubled but just for comparison let's more than double that figure for all the housing in the world making it 20,000 square miles. Using the DOUBLED figure, all the housing in the world easily takes up less than .038 %, which is almost 4/100ths of 1%. We are a very long way and many, many years from even using 1% of the earth's surface for housing the world population.

One may ask, "What about the mountains, deserts, cold regions and dense jungles?"

OK. I already more than doubled the space needed since 1970, now let's cut the available land in half. Now we are talking about almost 8/100ths of 1% for all the housing in the world ON HALF THE LAND MASS. Not much of difference, huh? I could keep doubling and halving and finally we would reach 1%. Are you following these calculations? Eventually we could pretend that all of the housing on earth could take up 1% of all the land surface by huge, sweeping changes like halving the earth's entire land mass several times and doubling the true number of houses on the planet several times.

Actually, all the railroads, paved roads, shopping centers, parking lots, industry, all types of paving, homes and buildings put together take up less than 1% of the earth's land surface. And I am still excluding Antarctica from these calculations. Antarctica isn't too livable anyway. America is far more developed than third world countries and the same statistic still holds up here. All the paving, industry and buildings combined do not use even 1% of our nation's land.

Not only does the incredible engineering in nature reveal wisdom, but it looks like there was no poor planning in the size or resources provided for all the creatures of the earth. There may be problems with man's greed or ignorance, but there is no shortage of resources.

Here is another amazing statistic that you can double-check on your calculator. If we say there are 5 billion people in the world, they could all attend one meeting in a huge ball ½ mile in radius, or one mile across (diameter).

What Overpopulation? Let's look at some more statistics. There is a saying, "*Figures don't lie, but liars work figures.*"

2 x 2 x 2 x 2 x 2 is multiplying the multiplication. The five two's in that equation go like this: 2 x 2 = 4, 2 x 4 =8, 2 x 8 = 16, 2 x 16 = 32, and 2 x 32 = 64. It's called exponential. Exponential growth is the same multiplication used to sell multi-level programs, get rich ideas and fear of "overpopulation." Overpopulation is my target. They have used exponential multiplication and scared the fertility out of people all over the world.

The *Zero Population Growth* people have convinced most of the world that we have a big overpopulation problem. They preach the doomsday stuff about not enough resources, not enough space, not enough food and that people need to have fewer babies before it's too late. It is an easy sell because, as stated above, most of the world population lives in and around cities. People see the expanding cities and the open fields vanishing. The *Zero Population Growth* people say the world population doubles every 37 years. Sounds scary, but we need to check the numbers.

If the world population doubled every 37 years, mankind would have to have just appeared on earth 1200 years ago to get to our present population. Don't believe me or them. Figure it out for yourself. Just double 2, then double 4, then double 8, etc. Do that 32 times and you will get 4,294,967,296. It only takes 1,184 years to make 32 generations doubling every 37 years. Do you really think the first humans appeared just 1184 years ago? That would be the year 812, which is 750 years AFTER Christ. More than a thousand years after Alexander the Great conquered the world, and the Great Wall of China was completed.

Permit me to show you how to generate fear starting with true numbers but using true numbers falsely.

Let's use the growth rate of a baby. After conception, a child in its first month of life grows 10,000 times from its original fertilized size. At this rate, it will be 100 million times bigger than its original size by the end of the second month (10,000 x 10,000) (I see a sci-fi story forming— *Honey, Stop the Kid from Growing*).

You see, you take a real fact and then *project* from there and things can get extremely miscalculated. By the third month, at the first month's rate of growth, the baby would weigh 2,000 pounds. Gee, there goes mom's figure with a 2,000 pound baby inside at the end of her 3rd month of pregnancy.

For the sake of ridiculous… after 9 months, the baby would weigh more than the whole earth, using the first month's fetal growth rate.

It appears to any calculating person that the world is big enough and has enough resources to continue supporting man, animal, fish and plant life indefinitely. We even yield more per acre today than we did 50 years ago. The problem is not population but rather the way resources are allotted. Governments *pay* farmers to grow fewer crops to reduce the surplus even though the U.S. exports food more than anything else. There is no shortage of food, just generosity and lots of mismanagement.

If you have four people in a family and one person eats 60% of the food, you don't have a population problem. The problem may be that person. Or in another situation, the problem may be simply controlling waste or greed.

I have one more saying for you, "*The right diagnosis is 90% of the cure.*"

More productive taxpayers developing undeveloped land and buying more products and putting more money into economy and Social Security is a good thing. This is not a political statement.

Population growth helps people. Bad morality hurts people.

Conclusively, the design of the earth and available resources provides far more than we need. It looks like a well-planned planet to me.

INGENIOUS NO-BRAIN (MASTER DESIGN)

What about this idea that great ideas, real engineering, superb design, ingenious architecture and extremely complex interdependence is made and controlled by nothing?

The idea is like the scarecrow in Wizard of Oz... no brain.

Interdependence, Ecology, Biosphere, Symbiosis, Ecosystem and the whole idea of protecting our environment are all relatively new ideas recognizing the wisdom and importance of various systems working together. These are not new ideas in nature, but science recently discovering these old ideas that have been continually at work and inventing new words.

If you take a car apart and put it back together then find yourself with thirty parts leftover, chances are your car won't work as well, or possibly not at all.

Appliances in the U.S. use a different amount of electricity than appliances in Europe.

Different species work much the same way in all the environments throughout the world. You remove parts of nature and don't know what else it may affect. This reveals a master design.

Not only are there thousands and millions of amazing, highly engineered parts, but these parts work together. They are connected. They are dependent on one another. They are part of a whole.

Creatures function well in their own habitat.

It is like car parts. Chevy parts were made for Chevys and Ford parts were made for Fords. Some parts are interchangeable, most are not.

If you transplant a species into a different environment, it may fail to thrive or have no natural enemies and become a plague to its new environment.

If you need a nut and bolt, it has to be a nut and bolt that fit together and into the piece it holds.

Every species seems custom-made for the particular environment it is in. This includes animals, plants, bugs and even fungus.

Fish don't drown. Trees get nutrients out of the dirt. Plants make food from the sunlight. Birds eat bugs. The huge blue whale eats tiny plankton. Beavers cut down trees to build dams.

Wouldn't it be stupid if trees needed nutrients NOT found anywhere? Wouldn't it be dumb if beavers lived where there was no wood? Wouldn't it be ridiculous if plants had everything to make food except one missing unavailable ingredient?

Of course, the species would be an accident and perish in its first generation. It wouldn't deserve to be called a "species." "Fluke" would be more appropriate.

Numbers from December '94 issue of Popular Science

Vertebrates are creatures with backbones. There are 45,000 species of vertebrate on the planet.

There is an additional amount of undiscovered species estimated at 50,000!

Insects known and documented – 950,000, but 8–100 million yet undiscovered.

Algae known – 40,000 but 200,000 to 10,000,000 undiscovered.

Plants known – 250,000 but 3–5 hundred thousand undiscovered

Crustaceans (critters with shells like crabs) 40,000 known, but 150,000 undiscovered

Viruses known – 5,000, but perhaps 500,000 undiscovered

Spiders & mites – 75,000, but 750,000 to 1 million undiscovered

Bacteria – 4,000, but 200,000 to 10 million undiscovered

Every single one of these species can reproduce. Every one of these species *knows how to* reproduce. Every single one of these species knows what to eat and how to get it. Every one of these species know how and where to transport themselves if necessary. Every one of these species that needs a "house" knows how to find one or build one from its own instinct and surroundings. Every one of these species has the environment that provides the natural resources they need to survive.

Superior design, master design, massive design, consistent design, superior wisdom with order and complexity far above man's ability to copy or even comprehend…

Uncertain of the effects of a species going extinct, governments now protect them. What happens to the master plan if we pull out one piece?

UFO—IN TOLLHOUSE, CALIFORNIA?

There it was with no warning, darting back and forth with unearthly agility. People were staring at it in broad daylight. It appeared with regularity and the military was brought in to not only observe, but with the hopes of downing it with as little damage as possible.

Although not reported in the news, it was downed and rushed to top scientists for analysis.

Most witnesses saw the incredible maneuverability allowing the object to fly under wires and land with such precision as has yet to be designed into any man-made aircraft.

It could bolt right onto a crevice in a rock and land without a scratch or sound.

With ease, it plotted its way between trees and even branches of the same tree without a flaw or miscalculation.

Its ability to suddenly and silently change direction once, twice or more times was hard to grasp, even while witnessing it.

Now the scientists had it in their laboratory. The exterior was shiny black with a purple sheen. It had a grain, sort of, but its exact substance could not be duplicated. There was certainly superior design but hard to interpret.

The protrusions on four sides in one plane were obviously for its aerodynamic performance. They saw how it moved and theorized how the four protrusions worked together for sudden changes and directions, but how was it engineered?

There was no computer or wiring to be found, although there seemed to be a center connected to all other parts. They called it the "brain" of the vessel. But they could not truly comprehend, let alone duplicate that brain.

Hoping to discover a new fuel, they examined the craft for evidence. Again, after reaching theoretical conclusions they still could not duplicate the technology that lay before them in their multi-million dollar laboratory.

The object of their study did provide some inspiration for aircraft as implemented in many examples today. But even our latest and most sophisticated designs are pitifully primitive by comparison. Our fuel consumption is comparably massive. Air agility technology is backward in contrast to this specimen. Our computers and electronics are bulky and aboriginal next to the extremely efficient network of monitoring and control of the alien representation.

Where did it come from? How embarrassing for the scientific community to admit they cannot duplicate, to this day, the technology; even with the sample in their clutches and 100% readily available for their research.

Since then, many other models have been made and additional specimens procured. Some are on display in museums around the world. And there have been recent sightings in Tollhouse.

You see, the flying model... is a bird; in this case, a crow.

STONEHENGE VERSUS THE UNIVERSE

My youngest son had the great privilege of going to see Stonehenge in person. It is a very revered and protected site. People from all over the world come to see this wonder of human intelligence from an unknown time period.

Theories abound. There is little disagreement about its use of the stars and sun to calculate. However, there is more controversy about whether it was used for a sacrificial site, pagan religious services or put there by visiting aliens.

There is plenty of discussion on intelligence other than our own modern wisdom. We assume we are now the greatest intelligence the earth has ever seen. We have electricity, lights, cars, planes, spaceships, computers, cell phones, satellites, TV, lasers and the greatest microscopes and telescopes. It awes us when we discover human intelligence that stumps us.

Case in point: the pyramids of Egypt. There is no final verdict on how the ancient Egyptians were able to transport such huge rocks to the desert, cut them so exactly, and lift them so high.

Another case in point: Easter Island has those large, face-sculpted rocks that are obviously not from that island. How did they haul such massive weight over water?

Stonehenge is another example of ancient wisdom.

What do you think would happen if there was a group that began holding press conferences stating that it is ridiculous to believe Stonehenge was designed by men or aliens and they know conclusively that it is simply a natural part of the landscape?

Are you thinking what I'm thinking?

International outrage, name-calling and mockery in every media form. They would be the butt of all kinds of jokes on late night TV.

Why? Isn't anything possible? Most open-minded people who even listened to their reasons would quickly disassociate themselves from endorsement of such foolishness.

Why would it be considered ignorant? Because the likelihood of a group of similar rocks in a circle that clearly has some capacity to function in measuring astronomical calculations is practically nil. So unlikely is such organization occurring in a natural landscape that the majority of the educated world would never seriously consider it.

But do you know what? The grass that grows on the ground at Stonehenge is billions of times more organized. It is alive. It can reproduce. It doesn't just measure the movement of the sun it utilizes and interacts with sunshine to manufacture its own food. Grass grows roots in the correct downward direction and knows how to extract nutrition and moisture from the soil. It grows, dies and revives again in the spring. It has various functioning parts and millions of cells with very specific functions requiring energy and coordination with other cells and it disposes waste (oxygen) and draws carbon dioxide from the air. Every living cell is made up of billions of atoms that have their own consistent properties and work in perfect order.

Guess what? There is a small but vocal group that is saying highly sophisticated engineering displayed in nature requires no intelligence. Oddly, practically the whole world has no problem agreeing the grass required no intelligence to design, but the circle of rocks did.

Why not apply the exact same logic to the grass around Stonehenge as is used on Stonehenge?

Stonehenge—stacked, placed rocks required great intelligence to assemble, but grass, ah that can just happen.

Sounds like some pagan sacrifice of science to me.

How Can Instinct Be Smarter Than The Animal?

Through the years I have written numerous articles about some fascinating instincts. My dog that had never had puppies before had left her mother when she was still a pup, and never attended birthing classes, knew exactly what to do when her first litter of puppies began coming. I have seen puppies born maybe fifteen times in my life and have much more experience with puppies being born than my dog does, but my dog knows exactly what to do better than I do.

How is that possible? Yeah, I know it is called instinct, but how can an animal know better than a veterinarian what is best for her pups?

Birds fly south at the right time and back again in season. Monarch butterflies fly their course. Salmon leave the ocean to swim upstream back to their own little stream where they were born to lay their eggs. These creatures do not get lost and their timing is always right.

Birds build nests consistent with their species' unique manner. Without hygiene lessons animals know to groom themselves. Generation after generation, animals know what to do, how to do it, where to do it, when to do it; everything from eating, grooming, mating and building their home, to a million ways to escape, defend, trap or attack.

How are their instincts smarter than they themselves? How can the instinct actually be more reliable than the wisdom of the brain/mind of the animal? Where does that wisdom come from?

Example: A map "knows" more roads than I do because it was made by a group of people with all this information available to them. They printed it on the map I am viewing. Maybe the map itself is not as intelligent as I am, but the information on the map that is guiding me is the result and the evidence of intelligence I need and lack.

Example: A policeman knows nothing about delivering babies but is on a radio getting instructions from a doctor as he tries delivering a baby. The radio is not smarter than the police officer but the doctor directing him IS smarter when it comes to delivering babies.

The radio is equivalent to instinct. The policeman is performing beyond his own intelligence from the radio. But a greater intelligence is talking through the radio.

The map is also equivalent to instinct. I know what's ahead even though I have no experience or telepathic powers. The map guides me. The intelligence is not in the map but *through* the map from others who have greater knowledge and experience about these roads than me.

How else could it be possible that an animal can receive instructions through "instincts"?

Makes one wonder, huh?

REPRODUCTIVE DINNER

I know most of us are now too squeamish to kill our own chickens, pluck them, clean them and eat them. Most of us don't raise our own cow for a couple years and then kill our pet for weeks or months of beef products. Pigs, turkeys, lamb and a whole array of edible meat are things we buy in packages at the store.

The one thing that these animals have in common with vegetables and fruit is that they all have the ability to reproduce. That is very fortunate for us because we get hungry not only every day but several times a day. If we consumed just a pound of food a day (on the average) from day one to age 70 that's 25,550 pounds of food—more than 12 tons. How many cows is that?

As Americans, we probably throw away almost as much as that every day; leftovers nobody wants, fat cut off meat, stale bread, food in the fridge too long or just to make room for the food just purchased. This doesn't count the food thrown out at restaurants, butcher shops and grocery stores that are outdated or unused. And it certainly doesn't include the millions, if not billions of tons of food grown in fields and orchards that are never harvested for several reasons. Add to that the food that is harvested but thrown out because it doesn't meet criteria established by the wholesale buyers.

This idea came to me when watching a show about rabbits. They are chased and caught by so many kinds of animals, it is a wonder they are not extinct. They would be except for their most powerful weapon—reproduction. How sad for the little bunnies. They individually don't have any secret weapon to defend themselves from owls, cougars, foxes, coyotes, bobcats, snakes and a long list of predators on every continent except Antarctica. The TV program said the average life span in the wild is about 9 months. In my encyclopedia it says they live about 10 years. I assume that would be a pet in safe captivity. It is the rabbit *species, not the rabbit* that has the weapon of reproduction. Because of their breeding ability, without predators, they would quickly overpopulate an area and become a plague. Mama hares have 4–8 litters every year with 3–8 young in each litter. If we go halfway and say 5 litters of 5 baby bunnies every year for 10 years and the same for half of those (assuming half are female) it is more than 300 bunnies by the end of the second year and nearly 4,000 by the end of the third year. By the end of the tenth year, you have a rabbit problem—more than 186 billion, and that's starting with two rabbits.

But this article isn't about rabbits; it is about how fortunate we are to have food that reproduces. With more than 5 billion people in the world, it seems frightening to think about feeding all of us but if you do the math, there is easily more than enough food for much more than 5 billion. The starvation in our world is not from a lack of intelligent design but rather a combination of greed, politics, ignorance and sometimes the misfortune of weather or plague.

Even with our unending appetites and the billions of us continuing to reproduce, there is no need for concern because abundance is in place on a grand scale to not only feed us but make us fat.

With all the meat, fruits and vegetables in the world the variety and the pleasure of their taste, it is wondrous that it is the fuel for our amazingly designed body. Not only is intelligence required to set up something so complete, so large and so adequate, but when you consider the additional luxury of "taste buds," it seems pleasure has been generously granted for consuming the fuel that is vital to our physical survival.

IN THE KITCHEN

Alibrando's Law #4
Reproduction

UN-PROVABLE NOTION: All species are descendents of not one, but many different species and classifications of species (mammal with reptile ancestors descended from fish who descended from shellfish who are descendents of single-celled organisms).

SENSIBLE FACT: No species has babies that are a different species.

TECHNICAL WORDING: *No species is the origin of another species with a different number of chromosomes.*

The symbols below represent that each species reproduces exclusively its own species and does not reproduce any other species. This is easily proved in a laboratory. "A" reproduces "A," "B" reproduces "B," "A" does not have "B" babies.

A ⇨ A   B ⇨ B

A ⇎ B

EXPLAINING THE LAW

Do you know what creatures must have in common to reproduce with each other? They have to have the same number of chromosomes. Dogs and wolves have the same number of chromosomes so they can reproduce but even with artificial insemination, we can't make a puppy that is half cat. That is because they do not have the same number of chromosomes.

Although there are many species of animals, there is not a single *proof* that even one has emerged from a different species that has a different number of chromosomes.

While drawings and animations present the possibility, in all these years there is still not a single, solitary scientific observation of one species giving birth to a different species that continues on as a new species.

A deformity would not qualify as a reproducing new species. What science has observed is that when there is a major deformity, that specimen is usually unable to reproduce. It appears sterility is a precautionary measure invoked by the DNA to protect the species from reproducing major flaws—a type of quality control. Minor characteristic changes that are passed on to babies are minor characteristics not a new species.

Similarities in anatomy, does not give them the ability to reproduce with each other. For instance, a chimp cannot mate with an orangutan. An eagle cannot mate with a crow. The identical number of chromosomes is the key to permitting reproduction, so:

LAW #4
> *No species is the origin of another species with a different number of chromosomes.*

RELATED ARTICLES:
Reproductive Dinner

SCIENCE KEEPS PROVING HOW LITTLE WE KNOW

What gets me researching most of the time is a question. I observe something and then wonder, "How does that work?"

For instance, how do salmon know how to come back to the same tiny creek they were born in after swimming thousands of miles out to sea?

The next thing I usually do is look to science to see what they know about it. What's great about science is that it asks many of the same questions, but when it answers one it generates another ten questions.

Typically, the next ten questions require sophisticated equipment and a research grant. When all the experimenting is over, we can only marvel at the exceeding sophistication and complexity of overlapping and interlinking systems all too marvelous even for science to grasp, let alone duplicate.

Science repeatedly proves there is more intelligence in systems all around us than man has himself.

The greatest minds in the world, equipped with millions of dollars of equipment can't stop feet from smelling. We can't stop the rain. We can't stop earthquakes. We can't figure out how to make a single seed.

How is it we honor science as though they can do anything? Friends and loved ones die all the time in hospitals under the best care.

We can make airplanes fly but we can't create minds that can make airplanes fly.

We can see fantastic technology in TV but we can't make eyes that see.

We have the imagination to tell stories of traveling to far off galaxies but we still know very little about what's inside our own planet, let alone our own solar system.

We are like children who see just the outside of things with no understanding. A child knows a person as the "man with the big nose," the "fat lady" or the "ugly man." They have no real understanding of people. We are much like them when we look at nature.

We are learning what planets look like. We can make a glass eye, a toupee or change our bodies through plastic surgery. We can switch hearts, we can use a donor's kidney, and we can clone.

Copying the Mona Lisa doesn't make me an artist: Stealing a TV doesn't credit me for creating one: Cloning isn't creating.

Where do we get all this pride that tells us we are so smart?

We are much smarter than the animals but who made us?

WHODUNNIT?

When investigating a crime, the detective looks for evidence. Sure, he may have a hunch whodunit, but a good detective lets the facts steer him to conclusions. Let's make up a sharp detective named "Shelly."

We know only a bad detective ignores evidence because he wants his hunch to be true—PERIOD. Let's invent a bad detective and call this guy "Claude."

In our story, a clothing manufacturing building has been burned down. Claude is sure a guy named Antonio burned it down for money. Sharp Shelly thinks it's possible too because Antonio has done it before.

Both detectives start searching for clues. They both find out from witnesses, Antonio was out of town the night of the fire. But Claude (the bad detective) insists the witnesses were lying or mistaken. He doesn't want to believe them because he already said he thinks Antonio did it. So Claude invents a theory that Antonio may have hired a look-alike for his out of town alibi.

Police investigators report to both detectives that it was an electrical fire. Shelly and Claude both know Antonio always starts fires with kerosene, so Shelly (the good detective) is now persuaded Antonio probably didn't do it. Claude really doesn't want to be wrong so he figures Antonio must be changing his style just to throw the police off-track.

The plot thickens.

Both Shelly and Claude meet another witness who says he saw a man and woman run from the building just before the fire started. They show the witness a picture of Antonio. The witness says no way. He says the guy had more hair, was heavy and about six feet tall. Antonio is a short, skinny, bald guy. Sharp Shelly begins looking for the two suspects but Claude says Antonio must have been wearing a wig, stuffed himself with pillows, and got himself a girlfriend. Shelly confronts Claude about the difference in height. (Reader: Look what Claude says.) Claude says the witness was obviously mistaken since Antonio is short. (Are you noticing that any witness who provides evidence contrary to Claude's theory is "wrong"?)

Sharp Shelly accuses Claude of just wanting to put Antonio in jail for this crime and that Claude is not interested in the facts.

Shelly eventually tracks down the two suspects and arrests them. They even confess to the crime. Claude is humiliated but not willing to face facts. Claude comes up with another theory and tells Shelly, "Antonio must have threatened the couple or paid them both to confess to the crime." Shelly frowns at Claude and turns to pick up something. Shelly shows Claude a video that the guilty pair took of themselves committing the crime just to show their friends. Shelly then explains to Claude "It's the video that got the criminals to finally confess."

Did Claude finally admit he was wrong and congratulate Shelly? Nope. Claude shakes his head and says "I can't believe how expertly this tape was tampered with. It really makes it look like this couple did it instead of Antonio. Man, this Antonio is a genius. But he can't fool me. I know Antonio did it and I'm going to prove it.

Shelly drops his jaw in amazement at Claude's refusal to accept the plain evidence.

The End.

The moral to the story: You just can't convince some people no matter how much evidence you give them. They have their idea and no matter how much evidence piles up pointing to another conclusion. They brush it off.

Evolution, which I once considered fully credible, lost its appeal for me the more I learned. Specifically, the most obvious is that incredible engineering designing itself accidentally and without intelligence. From the realms of space, our precision solar system, to the huge effect of delicate weather when temperatures change by a few degrees, life in the oceans, forests, jungles and the intricate balance of dependence between so many forms of life. Do I go on? From galaxies to cells, molecules, atoms and electrons we find precise, consistent, often predictable but always amazingly constructed design.

To me, this design not only proves intelligence, but most of it surpasses all human intelligence. There are specialists in every field of science and medicine all trying to grasp so many things still unknown or understood – just in their own field of specialty.

But Claude still says it's all just an accident and he's gonna to prove he's right evidence or not.

In The Kitchen
Alibrando's Ripple 3 of Law #10
Suspicious Resistance to Evidence

The pebble is "An Expert Opinion is still an opinion and not a fact."

The 1st ripple is that no degree, certificate or endorsement keeps that person from making mistakes.

The 2nd ripple is about when experts start joining their opinions together or building on each others' opinions; it still doesn't turn opinions into facts.

This 3rd ripple targets the person or group that keeps rejecting facts.

UN-PROVABLE NOTION: Experts reject facts and evidence for good reasons.

SENSIBLE FACT: Rejecting evidence can be ignorant, but when an expert does it, it is suspicious.

TECHNICAL WORDING: *The more evidence an expert ignores, the more they prove they are against what is true.*

When there is nearly equal evidence for two sides of a debate, the subject is controversial. When there is overwhelming evidence on one side of a debate, the expert rejecting the evidence should become controversial.

The graphic below represents the correlation between someone saying "I don't believe it" even though there is lots of evidence. Why don't they believe it?

At the bottom of the graph you see a person who also says "I don't believe it" but there is no evidence so they shouldn't believe it. There is nothing suspicious about that.

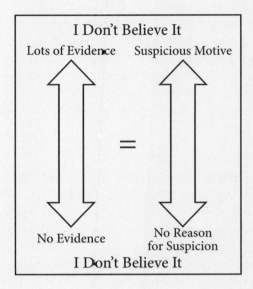

EXPLAINING THE LAW

If five umpires all see a play at a baseball game and four say he was out, why is one umpire saying he was safe? Show him the replay. All five review the replay and the four umpires say, "See?" and still the one says "Safe!" The focus moves from the play to the mysterious umpire. Why he is refusing to admit the obvious is anyone's guess.

The four umpires are not under suspicion because they agree with what they see.

Look again at the graphic. It is normal to not believe something that offers little evidence. That's Okay. It is rejecting something with overwhelming evidence that is suspicious.

The plainer it is and the less controversial the information is, the more suspicious the unbeliever becomes.

If you are presented with piles and piles of real evidence to believe something and because of that you do believe, why do other people presented with the same information say "I don't believe it"?

It could be any number of reasons that I do not wish to present here. It is clear, however, that they are closed-minded about the truth for some reason.

Emotions can cloud a person's judgment, but when a paid expert takes a stand against the evidence, it is almost criminal.

RIPPLE 3 OF LAW #10
> *The more evidence an expert ignores, the more they prove they are against what is true.*

RELATED ARTICLES:
Whodunnit?
Just Luck

100% PURE AND NATURAL
> "Grown without herbicides"
> "No preservatives added"
> "Just wheat and nothing else"
> "Organically grown"
> "The way nature intended"
> "Raised without… ?"
> "No genetic modifications or enhancements"
> "100% Certified Organic"
> "Earth-friendly"
> "Natural ingredients"
> "Non-toxic"
> "100% Pure and Natural"

It seems as though in the 30's, 40's and 50's manufacturers found ways to "improve nature" with whiter bread, whiter sugar, increased shelf life with preservatives, food coloring, etc. However, the more we learn about manmade "improvements" to our food the more the public demands untouched, unadulterated, untreated, unmodified natural food.

Hundreds of companies, in an effort to ride the trend, have falsely advertised their product as "natural" when in fact it was not. This created the need for manufacturers and growers whose products were truly without preservatives or other chemicals to convince an untrusting public that the "natural" or "organic" claim was real with them.

This led to third party certification. Separate organizations telling consumers, "This really is natural; We checked it out." It's kind of a consumer advocate group.

As would be expected some companies had the nerve to create their own certification, misleading the public to think they were certified by some third party as "natural and organic" but they simply certified themselves.

This is a big issue because the public does not want to be duped on what is truly 100% pure and natural.

The public continues to learn as science continues to investigate, that natural foods without preservatives, coloring, chemicals, insecticides or genetic modifications are safer, healthier foods. This is not news. It is general knowledge.

This is no new trend either. I remember quite a few hippie types selling organic food in plain brown wrappers in the 60's. Some of those guys are big-time corporations today but genuinely certified by 2–5 third-party organizations on their labels. Because the public has demanded true certification, there are many states that have implemented legal definitions as to what constitutes "organic" or "natural."

But think about this. With no religion or controversy, the general public is not just admitting but demanding that their health be protected by offering "natural" foods. This means *as nature designed it.* The public is largely resisting any "improvements" of science and commercialism and demanding that man-made inventions stay out of their food.

Who is nature? Whose knowledge of health, chemistry, organics, plants, horticulture, agriculture and diet created the "perfect" foods?

Once again, mankind is rallying to "nature" as the ultimate wisdom beyond anything man can invent or imagine. It is humans, the "ultimate intelligence of the universe," insisting on legal certification that the product they consume is in fact NOT "improved" by man. Consumers want to rest assured that what they are eating is in fact 100% natural and NOT tampered with by man's inferior wisdom.

The majority of research and public belief indicates that manmade attempts to improve food are usually a step backward or a step further away from health.

Here we go again, is anyone noticing the irony of this? The same public majority that believes there is no intelligence greater than man also believes there is no intelligence greater than nature. The same scientists that present evidence of natural foods being generally superior than manmade manufactured foods also believe nature is not "intelligently designed" but a result of unguided, random accidents. Do these guys bet on long shots at the horse races too?

I think it is hard to improve on honesty. An honest person just wants to know what is true. He has no agenda. He doesn't reject ideas just because they are contrary to what he previously thought was true. An honest man may not be necessarily happy to learn that he was wrong.

An honest man is happy to learn what is true INSTEAD of continuing to believe something wrong.

100% pure and natural honesty not colored with pride, not preserved with slanted agendas, not modified with boastfulness about never being wrong.

Maybe I should ask, "Could we really improve on 100% pure uncolored, unmodified, unrefined natural truth that doesn't need the preservatives of complicated PhD arguments which are over our heads and that most honest thinking folks don't really understand?" C'mon, are we really so gullible that we are supposed to believe things way, way outside our common sense? All man-made design requires thoughtful intention, but all design in nature does not?

THE ASSUMPTION

It's funny how whenever scientists study anything in nature they expect it to be organized, sophisticated, and wise.

This is no surprise to any reader but consider the implication. Scientists EXPECT great order and engineering beyond their own ability in nature. Scientists EXPECT and assume that all nature and every field of study from atoms, cells, skin, bones, instincts, weather patterns, astronomy, migration patterns, etc., is going to be smarter than the scientist himself. Scientists are not looking for design errors or random sloppiness in nature but instead they EXPECT to discover ingenious workings. They look for this in plants, animals, humans, and even non-living elements. They expect and assume that there is a reason why things do what they do. Consistently, if they study long enough, they find intelligent reason for why something is there—functioning, playing a role, having a purpose.

They predict that if they study it long enough they will learn the wisdom of the design. Often, the wisdom is far-reaching and affects other species or systems.

Scientists EXPECT this. Why do they expect it? Because of a 100% pattern of everything else they have studied. Once upon a time, doctors and scientists said the appendix was a useless organ leftover from evolution when we used to roam fields and eat grass. Whoops. They now know that was wrong. They said the same about tonsils. I even had a dentist tell me that about some teeth he wanted to pull out in the back of my mouth when I was 18. You can bet any scientist or researcher who says nature made a mistake will be proven to be the mistake maker himself.

Don't you find it odd that the same scientists that always EXPECT nature's inventions to be intelligent and worthy of researching would also claim it was, in fact, NOT intelligently designed? Is that weird to you? It is peculiar to me that I am expected to agree with a "scientific" conclusion that states that as a result of random events, nature has been far luckier than some guy winning every single lottery.

Would you get suspicious if some guy named Larry won every single lottery in California over and over for forty years and nobody else ever won? Never—nobody ever won except Larry. They would stop calling it the lottery and call it the Larry Contribution Fund. People would stop putting money in after a few weeks (probably much sooner) and anyone who did would be considered stupid. Who would believe anyone on a talk show saying, "It is a fair lottery—I think it is just incredible luck for one guy who keeps winning. Anyone can still win the lottery?"

"But Larry has won 146 lotteries in a row!"

"Lucky Larry!"

Then the next day Larry wins again. He continues monopolizing the next twenty-five lotteries, collecting every single prize. Would you think he was lucky or that the lottery was fixed?

The chances of Larry winning every single lottery his entire life is far, far more statistically possible than even *one* living species being designed by accident. Just *one*, not two, not ten, not a thousand, not a million, just *one*; even a bug.

To this day, all of man-made science combined cannot manufacture one living thing. Not a bug; not a living cell. There is nothing simple about their design. They are incredibly sophisticated. "Simple" is a joke to describe any life form. Yet we don't consider ourselves gullible when we say all of nature, life and the universe came into existence by luck; without a plan, a plot, any work, any design or any premeditated intelligence.

You would be suspicious if someone won the lottery three times in a row but we think we are not gullible to believe all life came about accidentally!

Me, I think the universe was fixed, a setup; on purpose. Yeah, you can't con me. I know a plan when I see one.

THE RELIGION THING

We often hear that religion is superstition. I've heard it said it has its source from primitive culture. Many declare it is the stuff for simple minds that know no better.

I've also noticed most religions credit some god for creating things.

Some have many gods. But how many psychological and scientific studies conclude religion has primitive, uneducated origins.

Animals, as far as I can tell, worship no god of their own species. For instance, ducks don't worship some duck king from ancient times. Monkeys really don't sacrifice to a monkey god in hope of a good banana season. We don't see cats gathering together to pray against all the dogs or making dog dolls to stick pins in.

If early man is the top of the "evolutionary chain" and he is the only species that is religious, how is religion primitive? In other words, if the only species on the planet that practices "religion" is the most intelligent species on the planet and all the species that do not have religion are only the less intelligent species, it seems we can associate religion with intelligence.

Maybe animals are too dumb to care about what they don't know. Maybe one of the greatest signs of intelligence is the discovery and conclusion that there are greater forces at work. We do not control everything. There are sophisticated principles and properties, far beyond what primitive or modern man could possibly control.

Maybe only intelligence recognizes greater intelligence. Maybe only intelligent creatures are curious about origins. It seems only the highest intelligent species (man) seeks personal meaning. Why am I here? What is my purpose?

Here is the question. If religion is a sign of intelligence, how should we classify humans that have no religion?

How seriously can we take those declaring that they are more intelligent because they don't believe in religion? All the animals don't practice religion. Religion is only practiced by the most intelligent species on earth—mankind.

Assume there are three creatures walking together on a deserted island. Two are primitive natives and one is a pet monkey. They stumble across a deserted apartment complex. The monkey sniffs it and moves on looking for food. One native reasons that the building grew there on its own. His logic is that it wouldn't be there unless it grew there and the fact that it is there "proves" it grew there. The second native recognizes intelligence. He examines the materials, the correct height of the doors for walking through. The perfect fit of the doors in the doorways. The windows that are clear and mostly the same size and at the same height seems more than coincidental to the second native. He sees that the window screens could keep out insects and the windows slide easily to be closed or open. The second native sees the symmetry of the stairs and how easy it is to walk up and down. He places his hand on the side rail and notices how it is at a comfortable height to lean on. He sees intelligence here. He sees design.

Who is the smartest of the three?

What should we say about humans who proclaim there is no superior intelligence while they are surrounded by natural engineering of superior intelligence (nature)? Should we agree it is all coincidence? Should we agree and marvel that more billions of organized systems and organisms than we can count are not the result of intelligence—but random luck?

Yes, it is true that all primitive cultures acknowledge that greater powers exist. Does this universal trait reveal ignorance or common sense?

Is it ignorant to believe in an intelligence source greater than our own? Is it naïve to admit there is intelligence so much greater than human intelligence or that we feel inclined to respect such great power and wisdom?

While we admit there are greater powers than man in our world, in our weather, in our bodies, in the instincts of animals, in space, in birth and death, we like to call it "science."

But what is more ignorant; to say these greater designs and powers required intelligence, or that they occurred without intelligence?

Invite any animal to a religious service and you will find it is of no value to the animal, but most people that have not been educated in evolution instinctively believe they are surrounded with evidence of great and superior power.

INVENTING ONESELF

What is missing in Nature?

Nothing I can think of except more natural enemies for mosquitoes and some way of restricting weather temperatures to 55–75 degrees and stuff like that.

We all know how nature does such a wonderful job at everything. Survival – balance – cells – reproduction – molecules – chemistry – orbiting planets – healing skin – critters that keep other critters population in balance – nervous systems – skeletal systems – circulatory systems – mating instincts – migration instincts and on and on.

Oh yeah, nature invents things, at least according to some theories. I got to thinking "How did nature invent *itself*?"

First, if I invented myself I would have to be way brainier than I am.

Can you make a heart like the one you have? Can you make eyes like the ones you are reading with? Can you personally make anything like the stuff that is working in your own body right now? You're way smarter than single-celled organisms and fish, right?

Wait a minute. Even if you or I could invent ourselves, how could we do that BEFORE we existed? Whoa dude!

You cannot invent yourself before you exist. You would have to exist in order to invent yourself so it just isn't possible. Now that we have ruled out the possibility of anything inventing itself, something before us had to invent us. Only something that already existed can invent something new. Only something that already existed can invent somebody. Mom and dad didn't invent us. They did what comes naturally but they can't make brains and organs even if they are surgeons or scientists. So who invented the all-intelligent smarter than everything Nature? Well, certainly not Nature because we know nothing, including nature, can invent itself.

Yeah, who invented Nature? Who invented DNA? Who invented animal instincts? Who invented the coordination of various eco-systems, interdependent life and reproduction? What about floating, orbiting planets? Who invented the natural laws of nature that dictate how all this stuff works? Who invented the natural laws of science that we know about and all the laws we have yet to discover?

I don't expect an answer to all these questions, I only pose this main point for you to consider—since nothing can invent itself.

How Long To Make 6 Billion People?

Do you think within 40 years a couple could have four children? Do you think it is reasonable that 100 people could have 200 kids within 40 years?

For most of history, having many children was smart because it represented more help on the farm, more help working the ranch, more strength, a bigger tribe, more soldiers, more protection, more women, more wealth.

It is sometimes surprising to learn the things we can actually figure out for ourselves.

I want to give you a formula. If you do not agree with my numbers, you can just change them to whatever suits you using the same formula.

In my lifetime, the world population has doubled.

Generally, people accept a "generation" as 40 years.

For the purposes of this very interesting calculation, I am going to assume the population doubles every 40 years. On a piece of paper (if you're using a calculator) or on a spreadsheet, make a column on the left and write the numbers 1 to 34.

The approximate population in 2004 was 6 billion. Let's look to 2010 and round up the population to 8 billion. In the 2nd column next to "1" write 2010. In the 3rd column write 8,000,000,000. That's it, 3 columns. The 1st counts our generation as "1" in year 2010 having a population of 8 billion.

Here's what we want to do: go backwards 40 years and make it HALF the population (4 billion in 1970) and then back another 40 years to 1930 (2 billion) and of course, back to 1890 at 1 billion. You get the idea. By doing this you will find yourself going down to zero around the year 690 AD. This is the Middle Ages, which is after the Roman Empire and the beginning of the Byzantine Empire. The Tang Dynasty is flourishing. We can prove this history. That is only 34 generations—34 generations!

We can mathematically calculate our population backwards to zero in less than 1500 years. We have historical evidence that there were people here 1500 years ago.

Change whatever you want. Assume it takes 50 years to double the population or assume it only takes 20. Make a generation 30 years or 60 years if you want. More babies died at childbirth but people had more babies.

What you will quickly see is the impossibility of having millions or billions of years to go from 8 billion down to zero.

Sure, there were plagues and wars. Factor in whatever you want. You will find it impossible to take today's evidence and work backwards to one million years—and completely give up on 1 billion years.

Hey, where do they get these big numbers of millions or billions of years if we can believably go from 2 people to 8 billion people in just 34 generations? The answer is THEORIES; all kinds of theories—including dating methods built on theory. I don't mean dating and romance, I mean measuring the age of things—dating them. I did a prior article on this, regarding the fact that rings in trees are provable sources of counting seasons and years.

Without writing another article on dating, let me say that practical answers ought to also be considered like this simple math question of counting backwards. Let's hear theories that use evidence instead of so many theories that contradict evidence.

What if our earth is very young compared to what we have been told?

Is that a problem? If it is a problem, for whom is it a problem? Why would the truth be a problem, if it were true?

I think a curve ball is thrown at us by telling us common sense and our ability to reason should be ignored. This notion that over billions and billions of years anything could happen and science has nothing to do with it is goofy. Why should we leave this to theorists and not challenge them? Sure, some have invented theories that may be fascinating but sometimes totally unrelated to the good old scientific method, which is specifically there for proving or disproving theories.

Reader, you do the math. Apply the science. Test the theories against these and reach your conclusions based on the evidence. Whether 34 generations or 66 or even 200 generations, you just cannot fill a million years based on evidence or known history.

It's definitely something to at least be thinking about.

MISSING POPULATIONS

Consider the difference between ancient civilizations and comparatively young America. In the Mideast are ancient cities with multiple layers of different cities one on top of the other. Ruins with different civilizations buried deeper than a newer city and then another city on top of that.

In the U.S., as far as *human* culture, we have found only Indian history before Europeans settled here. In the U.S. 800 years is ancient. In parts of Europe and the Mideast ruins from 1,000 years may be the *top* layer with a city in the same place 3,000 years beneath.

It is tangible evidence of cities and civilizations uncovered by archeologists and placed in museums for all to see.

Scientists tell us dinosaurs lived before man and we have many proofs of those dinosaurs throughout the world and the United States. Why would there be hundreds of times the evidence of dinosaurs that supposedly lived millions of years BEFORE the caveman and yet little or no evidence of cavemen civilizations?

Things like cities, artifacts and dinosaur skeletons are hard evidence. Saying there were entire civilizations that roamed the earth for millions of years ought to leave some traces don't you think?

What do primitive drawings in caves prove? I am a terrible artist. If I tried to draw a hunting expedition on the wall, you'd think someone prehistoric drew it too. Even today, there are primitive cultures that make drawings on rocks. How does someone's IQ or ability to read, write or draw reveal the age of the earth? It doesn't. I see guys with slanted foreheads today.

Do you realize scientists are still looking for the missing link? They are still looking for that ONE skeleton that will "solve their case" to prove there was a species that evolved between monkeys/gorillas and man. They are still looking for ONE skeleton that is supposed to remove all doubt.

I am not talking about one caveman to prove an ethnic group but an *entire species*. We humans, as a species, have many ethnic groups. What if I told you there was an undiscovered ethnic group called IGRONESH. Not Caucasian or Latino or Negro or Asian, but a completely different ethnic group with unique features. I posed this question to my daughter when she was in Junior High. "How many skeletons would they have to find to satisfy you that such an ethnic group actually existed; 10 – 100 – 500 – 1000 – 10,000 –100,000?" She said 500. My junior high school age daughter felt she would be satisfied that an entirely separate, extinct ethnic group existed if they found 500 skeletons proving it—I guess for her 400 was not enough and 600 was not necessary.

I then explained to her that this was not the existence of a mere city or country but an entire ethnic group; a group that no longer exists but lived for thousands or millions of years. She then changed her answer to 1,000. I assured her that 500 were probably reasonable enough.

We aren't missing just a link, we are missing *populations!* There is a huge oddity about finding evidence of pre-caveman dinosaurs but no evidence of millions of years of caveman civilizations that "only lived after the dinosaurs."

We are missing not only links, but logic, time, and in my opinion, ought to finally move on to some more reasonable theories. You know, theories we can eventually prove scientifically.

Oh, and for the record, there are fossils of human footprints and they are right next to dinosaur footprints. You can see them for yourself, right here in the United States in Texas. They are not ape footprints or some modified version of human footprints but simply normal, human footprints. There is a trail where there are 134 dinosaur footprints crossing a series of 14 human footprints. There is even one spot where a human footprint is literally across a dinosaur footprint. All of these are near the Paluxy River near Glen Rose, Texas. It is tangible evidence. Look it up yourself.

But that aside, I think there ought to be a little more evidence than ONE missing link to convince the world such creatures roamed the earth for millions of years. Don't you?

THE THREE LITTLE PIGS

Which of the three little pigs was the smartest? The wolf blew down the straw and stick house but the third pig saved the day with his brick house, chimney and all.

Without an IQ test or knowing anything about the three little pigs, we all agree who is the smartest because of the best talent in architecture and building.

Let's take three more architects and you decide who is the smartest.

1. *Monkey* can use tools to break open a coconut.
2. *Man* can make airplanes, computers, skyscrapers, satellites, TV, radio, short wave and microwave communications. He can also make plastic plants, glass eyeballs, toupees and perform plastic surgery.
3. *Unnamed intelligence* can make birds, mountains, human brains, can invent moons, planets, universes, galaxies, millions of reproducing species that grow, eat and function interdependently. It can also make real plants and trees, eyes that see, ears that hear, hair that grows and skin that heals.

Now if you read science books and watch educational TV, usually they will tell you there is hardly a difference between #1 and #2. As far as looks and physical traits go, I guess I agree but as far as ability goes, I don't think there is any competition. And yes, I did see Planet of the Apes but I haven't read one book written by a monkey yet.

Most of these same educational programs will suggest that #2 is the greatest intelligence known in the universe and we are sending out signals looking for intelligent alien life. If you look again at number three, even without an IQ test but simply based on the architecture and building, I'd say number three is far smarter than #2. Just like I think a brick house with a chimney is plenty of proof of intelligence. Don't you? Still, these educational books and programs keep telling us it takes intelligence to make a straw house (monkey with a tool). They tell us it takes intelligence to build a stick house (man's inventions) and that we are the supreme intelligence. But, they teach our children and us, it takes absolutely no intelligence to make a brick house (everything in the universe). It just happened over billions of years by accident.

I'm sticking with the three-pig logic. The third pig proved he is the smartest by what he built. Show me one house that built itself accidentally and I'll show you a wolf that blows down houses.

IMITATION IS THE HIGHEST FORM OF FLATTERY

An imitation is something derived or copied from an original.

Very few of us have original paintings by Leonardo da Vinci but there are many copies. The copies are far less valuable but it is flattering to be able to sell not only your paintings but many copies.

Any artist who says, "I paint like Leonardo da Vinci" will never be as great as da Vinci because he is a copycat.

We live in a world of imitation.

Imitation grass, imitation crabmeat, and billion dollar industries in fields marketing things that look like the real thing.

In the medical field, we have false teeth, plastic surgery, plastic knees, prosthetic appendages, toupees, wigs, glass eyes and more, all trying to look real and natural.

In Botany, we have plastic and silk plants, trees, shrubs and flowers. The dentist's office I am in right now has paintings of flowers and fields in each office and along the hallways.

Much of the toy industry is "pretend stuff" like toy planes, trucks, guns, babies, cell phones, binoculars, tools, etc.

We try to imitate nature, but we are like children that can only pretend; glass eyes that don't see, plastic skin that doesn't heal, false teeth that need glue, toupees that fly off, expensive arms and legs that lack the qualities that the real leg had.

Someone once said to me that man can now create as much as nature because of cloning.

That is like cutting a piece of a da Vinci painting out, sticking it on my canvas, and claiming to be a great artist. Cloning is taking the original work of nature and moving it around. Genetics is the same. No one is creating anything. They are taking the original work of nature and manipulating it.

Yes, we are like kids pretending when it comes to copying nature. Who wouldn't want their real leg back? Who wouldn't prefer seeing eyes to glass ones? Who wouldn't prefer their hearing ears to expensive hearing aids?

Even though everything is right in front of us and all of science to copy with the help of microscopes, great technology, computers, and building on the research of others—we can't even begin to understand all the wonderful things that work around us. The technology in nature is so far superior to all of our combined science that we cannot grasp the technology well enough to reproduce it… but we can make nature toys… imitations that can't do what the real thing can.

So if imitation is the highest form of flattery, who are we flattering? Trillions of accidents over billions of years, with no intelligent help, that created technology beyond all of humankind's combined intelligence?

Aw, c'mon, who *are* we flattering?

IN THE KITCHEN

Alibrando's Law #11
Deference

UN-PROVABLE NOTION: Man is the ultimate intelligence and there is no evidence that there is any intelligence greater than his.

SENSIBLE FACT: We are students of nature.

TECHNICAL WORDING: *When any technology is studied, it is the inferior learning from the superior.*

Below, the graphics represent an action that always represents the type of relationship.

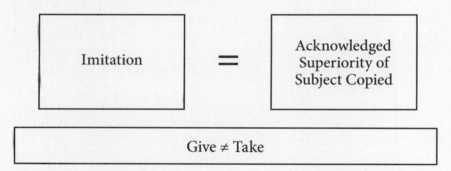

EXPLAINING THE LAW

Imitation is the highest form of flattery. A glass eye is inferior to a seeing eye. A plastic plant is inferior to a growing, living, reproducing plant.

Example 1: If you are an artist and envy another artist's work and style, you may find yourself attempting to imitate that artist's work. That is a compliment to the artist. If you successfully imitate that artist, you will be pleased with yourself. You will consider your current work superior to your former work. If you are unsuccessful, you are likely to remain somewhat envious of the ability of the artist you consider so great, so "superior."

Example 2: Let's say you are an inventor trying to invent a laser with unique properties. After years, you still keep failing but find out someone else has succeeded. You would want to learn from them to see what it is you missed. You would want to try to see if you could copy it.

If people want to copy you, you should be flattered. If you want to copy someone else, you must realize imitating them is a true nod of respect to their work. You will NEVER try to copy anything or anyone you consider inferior to yourself or your work, except to mock.

The copycat is the "student" and that being copied is the "teacher." One is asking questions the other is giving answers.

This is what baffles me. Nearly every field of science is a copycat studying a subject in nature and trying to learn how to either understand it or copy it. Every scientist is the student with nature being the teacher. It is the inferior studying a superior. No wonder, because there are so many technologies working so wonderfully in the human body and all of nature.

Here are similar relationships:

Inferior/superior, lesser/greater,
wanna be/already is, copycat/original
and in computereeze—upload/download

Nature is not studying man to learn from him. Man is studying nature to learn from it.

Nature continually holds that prominent position of being constantly imitated for the simple reason that it is superior. So, I would propose this plain and simple law:

LAW #11
When any technology is studied, it is the inferior learning from the superior.

RELATED ARTICLES:
Imitation is the Highest Form of Flattery

JUST LUCK?

If I personally know a guy who can design and build a TV and I refuse to admit he's smarter than I am, I have a problem.

It's bad enough that I have to admit he's smarter than I am why should I make myself look even dumber and say it's just an accident that he can design a TV? Undeniably, he can do something better than I can and that is design a TV.

Are you having a hard time believing everything in the universe is just a product of TRILLIONS of incredible accidents?

We can make false teeth, but we can't make real teeth. We can graft skin on burn victims from other parts of their own body, but we can't make real skin for them. We can put a pin in someone's broken leg but we can't manufacture a brand new bone or working leg that is anywhere close to as good as their original.

Isn't it extremely obvious that someone is smarter than we are? Would we rather look even dumber and argue that no one is smarter than our scientists are? Even the combination of all the knowledge of all our scientists can't manufacture most of the simplest things in our bodies, not to mention the rest of the planet and universe.

This doesn't have to be a religious question, or even a philosophical one. This is math.

If someone beats you at chess once, that might be luck. But you are just a bad sport if after losing ninety-nine times in a row you still say it's just luck.

If there was just one or two things that existed showing intelligent design superior to man's intelligence we might call it luck, but if there are hundreds, thousands, millions, billions, and trillions and we call it "luck" aren't we being pretty poor sports too?

All around us is design far superior to man's ability to even copy, much less create, and manufacture.

Do we continue debating that we are the supreme intelligence of the universe?

C'mon, that's just poor sportsmanship.

MAN, AN INTELLIGENT ANIMAL?

We see the chimpanzee and think of how much it reminds us of a child. We see a gorilla and think how it looks like one mean guy to tangle with. We watch educational TV and they tell us how certain apes use tools. We learn how other primates use sign language, and the message is "See, this is our heritage. This is our beginning."

We are like the animals in many ways, especially mammals. We bleed. They bleed. We have babies. They have babies. We have eyes, ears, brains and so do they.

Physically, we aren't much different, really. Scientists can go on studying the similarities and keep finding more for years, and I believe those physical similarities are there because I see them too.

However, there is another level that makes humans much different from animals, we seem like aliens from another planet by contrast. The difference is something you can't feel or weigh. It is something you cannot see under a microscope. Still, the evidence is plain. It is more than plain. It is overwhelming. Although the size and weight of the human brain and the size and weight of the brain of some primates are close, all comparisons end here.

Allow me to begin with the inventions of man. Out of the mind of man has come international communication via telephone, radio, TV, short wave and satellites in orbit around the world. Where is the similarity between us and animals in this realm? Men have studied physical laws in order to design helicopters, airplanes, jets, spaceships, and far-reaching satellites to study the planets. Where is even a primitive comparison of any intelligent animal? We have created submarines, automobiles, skyscrapers and computers. The physical difference seems so slight and yet the intellectual difference is tremendous. Our quest for energy and power has uncovered electricity, atomic power, gigantic river dams, windmills, solar power, engines powered by gas, oil, steam and batteries. The difference in our mental ability compared to all animals is immeasurable. To fight disease we have developed hundreds of vaccines. We have libraries filled with the research and sharing of information, stories, feelings and philosophies of centuries. What animals have accomplished anything near these achievements? Name one book written by a monkey.

Just the results of man's research alone, puts us in a totally different ballpark in the realm of intellect. It is not a mere ounce in weight that is important. It is the functional ability of man's mind. An ape using a rock to break something is not comparable to the intellect of man.

Would you say a round rock that can roll down a hill must be the ancestor of cars and evolved into a car because cars have rolling wheels? It is silly.

Psychologists, behaviorists, biologists, anthropologists and street corner experts like to tell us we are animals. We learn how we have instincts carried over from when we were apes in the fields but there is something in the human brain that we cannot find. We cannot physically account for the colossal superiority in human intelligence.

To me, far more significant is the spiritual difference of humans to animals. With animals, survival is not just everything; it appears to be the only thing. Species that mate for life don't do so for moral reasons but have internal *instincts* that govern their behavior. Some birds migrate, some don't. It is not morality or philosophy that governs animals, it is instinct.

On the other hand, to most people, survival is not enough. People seek happiness in hundreds of ways. People with enough food, clothing and shelter find themselves depressed and sad even though their survival is assured.

People have a strong motivation to understand WHY THEY ARE HERE. Individuals seek a meaning and purpose in life. The morality and belief of people are vitally important.

One group of humans will kill another group—not for food, shelter or survival—but because they didn't believe the same way. Animals don't kill creatures because they think differently. Throughout history human blood has been spilled in religious wars, political wars, wars of revenge, wars of greed and wars for power.

People have the unique capacity to be much more cruel and destructive to their own species and to other species, even when it is of no benefit.

On the flip side, people have virtue. National Geographic has never shown us a herd of elephants traveling great distances to bring food to a starving herd of elephants in another country. Monkeys in South America don't weep for the tragic end of the rainforests in Africa. People do. Gorillas don't pray for other gorillas in the community or around the world. People do. Baboons don't form clubs to help crippled or blind baboons. Wolves don't set up orphanages for pups whose parents were slaughtered in a distant land. Dolphins don't campaign for whales because they are close to extinction.

Humans are so totally different from all species of the animal kingdom; it almost seems like we are merely wearing earthly costumes to look like we belong to this world.

What *is* our purpose? How can we be so exceedingly above the whole of the animal kingdom? How can we be so superior, yet so pathetically inferior to the intelligence that designed the animals, birds, reptiles, and ourselves? We cannot even duplicate a seed that can grow, live and make more seeds. All of nature is a teacher that we still don't understand but know is wiser than we are. With outer space so large and our solar system so small, why are we here?

APPENDIX

A Few Observations
Unfortunate Human Tendencies

1. Popular Science Fiction: If everyone already believes a theory there is no need to prove it.

2. Popular License: If an unproven theory is popular enough, presenting it as true is no longer propaganda but education.

3. Grant Money Favoritism: Whoever controls the grant money for scientific projects decides what is scientifically important and what is a waste of money.

Good Cons

4. The Intellectual Con: Confusing conversation and intentionally talking over people's heads proves superior intelligence.

5. The Con of Presumptive Evidence: If a popular theory cannot be proven, it is not because it isn't true but because the "evidence remains hidden."

6. THE CON OF PRESUMPTIVE FICTION: If an unpopular theory seems to have evidence, it is not because the unpopular theory is true but simply "the correct interpretation remains hidden."

7. THE CON OF MONEY YIELDS PROOF: If a popular theory cannot be proven, it is only because more money is needed.

RULES
FOR SCIENCE
THAT MAKE SENSE

INTRODUCTION TO RULES for SCIENCE
(That ought to be enforced)

There is no need for rules unless there is misconduct. When something is abused, when people are taken advantage of or misled, rules need to be made.

Let the reader understand that in this book the "Laws" are laws like gravity and are always true. That is my claim. The Laws are observations of properties that cannot be broken.

RULES, as used here, are a prescription for conduct. They are boundaries, like speed limit laws can be broken, so can these RULES.

Naturally, those with dishonest motives figure out ways to bend the rules or get as close as possible to technically not stepping over the line. The dishonest may step over that line hoping no one notices they have stepped over the line.

Still, the rule itself is useful for alerting us that there is a problem that ought to be regulated. I believe it is very sad when a regular guy like me publishes in a book the obvious violations of these things that should never be violated in the scientific quest for knowledge. Like a legislator, a congressman, a school board member or a parent complaining to the school board, I think something should and can be done. I honestly don't know who can regulate these things if the scientists are not willing to police themselves. Still, schools and universities ought to see the importance here. The more the public knows, the better it is for all of us.

Contained in the next couple of pages are just a few proposals of some things I think should be regulated.

I am not asking you to go out and do anything other than consider the soundness of these standards.

Here is the format:

1. Rule Title
2. Rule
3. Who the rule is for primarily
4. Who benefits from the rule
5. Explanation of the problem

Rules For Science

Alibrando's Rule #1 -The Scientific Method Rule
No experiments, no proof, no conclusion.

FOR: Scientists publishing their findings and journals that publish the work of scientists or websites, etc.
BENEFICIARIES: All scientists who build on the work of others or whose work is undermined because they wrongly assume they are building on valid assumptions when it may be completely wrong.

This should not have to be a rule because it simply restates what real science has already stated. Unfortunately, it is necessary because it has become so common to ignore the rules of science in some fields.

The entire **scientific method** permits publishing the details of experiments so other scientists can duplicate the experiment and verify the validity of the conclusion. This is a simple and fantastic way of scientific accountability.

In the realm of science, what is a conclusion without experiments? Answer: An opinion.

The **scientific method** is the basis of the entire realm of authentic science.

Example 1: Good Science
A scientist has a theory and states his hypothesis. He defines the details of his experiment. He conducts his experiment and observes the results. Finally, he states his conclusions BASED ON THE RESULTS.

Other scientists verify his work. Science can then advance as other scientists BEGIN from this VERFIABLE scientific conclusion and expand from there.

Example 2: Bad Science Challenged by Good Science
If other scientists are given the details of the experiment and find differ-

ent results they are obligated to publish their contrary results. The first scientist has been challenged. The controversy draws interest; others test the theory with the same experiment and they may all agree the original scientist's conclusions are wrong. Now science is not polluted with false assumptions and true science prevails.

Example 3: Bad Science is Not Science
This should be "against the rules" but has become very common. In another scenario, a scientist states his hypothesis but says he cannot prove it through any experiments. He still makes conclusions anyway. He publishes his "expert" conclusions based on his personal observations and theories.

Other scientists cannot test his conclusions because he offers no way to test his conclusions. Those who assume his expert conclusions are true BEGIN to expand on his unproven theories and speculate further creating a growing network of assumptions based on assumptions.

Conclusions reached *without* experimentation cannot be re-proven by others (scientific method) and is therefore by definition **not a scientific conclusion**.

What is missing here? True science, the scientific method.

We can start a religious cult, a political conspiracy or any primitive local superstition using these same methods. Eventually, we reinforce all this with bandwagon peer pressure.

Therefore, the restatement is necessary:

RULE #1 THE SCIENTIFIC METHOD RULE
   No experiments, no proof—no conclusion.

Alibrando's Rule #2 - Science and Theory Separation Rule
Science shall be clearly separated from theory.

FOR: Publishers in every media format; teachers, professors etc.
BENEFICIARIES: The public at large. Also students, teachers, professors and scientists under the instruction of published material, professors or other scientists.

We may never be able to totally provide 100% accuracy in news reporting or history books, but there is usually a clear difference between what has been proven and what has not been proven. Why should the public and even scientists not be told the difference?

This rule applies to what is published. All media and public presentations ought to honor what is represented here.

This applies to scientists publishing their work, science journal publishers, scientific magazine publishers, nature publishers, all scientific school textbook publishers and the entire education media including TV, radio, educational aids and teachers.

This rule is needed because of the constant flaunting of theories and assumptions as "science." Whether it is done intentionally or not is irrelevant. It is irresponsible to mislead.

When a child hears his parent tell him something, he assumes it is true.

Often, when a person reads the newspaper, he assumes it is mostly true.

When a religious man quotes the Holy Word, listeners assume he is not misquoting it.

When a teacher speaks, students assume what is spoken is correct.

When a textbook or scientific journal is read, it is assumed to be true.

Certainly, when something is believed to be true for several generations it is even less scrutinized and becomes culturally accepted.

What is terribly misleading today is the overwhelming mixing of unproven theory with scientific fact creating science fiction posing as science.

In literature there is a genre called "Historical Fiction." This is using true historic events as a backdrop to fictional characters, relationships, etc. It has the feel of true, it has true events occurring throughout the story, but it is a fictional story.

There is no such clarification in science.

With this sloppy and constant mixing of fact and theory students, doctors, scientists and the public build on false assumptions, unintentionally.

The right way that a scientist or student builds a theory should be based on scientific evidence. That theory may or may not be correct, but at least it is attempting to build on true science.

If we build a theory based on a hybrid of theory and science our mental architecture is becoming wobbly. Too many variables are in the experiment. The basis is not even scientific.

This scenario is actually happening in some scientific circles. If we build theory on top of theory on top of theory; we are decisively leaving the scientific realm and entering into a franchise of fantasy. It is like discussing the scientific properties of the beanstalk in Jack and the Beanstalk. It is like discussing whether or not vampires can be seen in a mirror. It is like researching whether or not the pot of gold at the end of the rainbow is worth as much with inflation. Building multiple layers of scientific theory on top of unproven theories is simply designing superstition based on ideas that become culturally acceptable even though unproven.

Since ethics has not been enough motivation, I propose that rules ought to be declared. I believe students, scientists and the public desire to know which is fact and which is still unproven theory. We are all entitled to at least know the difference. Don't you think you, the reader, are at least entitled to know which is which?

There is no controversy, and *should not be* any controversy, regarding what is theory and what is science. One is provable using the scientific method; the other is not provable and is merely assumed or deduced.

RULE #2 - SCIENCE AND THEORY SEPARATION RULE
Science shall be clearly separated from theory.

Submitted for Your Consideration

A. **The Entitlement** - All those who desire to clearly understand and mentally separate proven science from unproven theories should have the benefit of this separation.

B. **The Rule** - All scientific journals, publications and textbooks should be required to put all unproven theories in italics or some unique, distinguishable font, so readers will not be misguided in their critical thinking. Radio and visual media would be required to insert clarification, much like drug companies are now required to state possible side-affects of drugs.

C. **Non-Compliance** - All print media that refuses to comply with this rule shall be required to state on the book cover and/or cover page that they refuse to separate theory and fact for the reader, according to the mandate. For non-print media, such announcement as to not adhering to this mandate shall be displayed conspicuously throughout the presentation or material also declaring that "We refuse to separate theories from proven facts in this presentation."

D. **Enforcing Authority** – I really don't know. Possibly the science community. (Or is this fox guarding the henhouse?) A science committee answerable to state or federal committee? Enforcement could be financed with a bond, and later with fines or from cost of textbooks or some other "tax." Those out of compliance (publishers, programs and learning institutions) should be warned and their refusal to separate theory from proven fact should be published. If there is some ongoing diligence to not comply either funding could be stopped, grants withdrawn or… ? Why should anyone, especially teachers, learning institutions or scientists intentionally refuse to stop misinformation and confusion?

Alibrando's Rule #3 - The Moving Forward Rule
Science should spend conspicuously more time building on what is true (proven) than trying to disprove evidence contradicting theories.

FOR: Scientists and researchers asking for funding of any kind (The private sector has no problem here because they won't tolerate waste).
BENEFICIARIES: Taxpayers, charitable donors, United States of America, all nations sharing scientific knowledge and research, the progression of science.

This rule is for redirecting all scientific fields in a fact-finding direction rather than a defensive standstill protecting opinions.

Historically, generations of the gullible public has been wooed away from scientific evidence or other truth using these persuasive methods:

A) Burning heretics and witches
B) Putting curses on those who disagree or challenge authority
C) Threatening
    1) A curse
    2) Ruined reputation

a) Expose you as evil

b) Expose you as stupid

c) Expose you as politically incorrect

Scientific progress is made by building on proof or working technology. This continues exponentially in the computer world. Where money is made by selling useful technology, the field of computer technology is not interested in theories that keep failing. There is nothing to build on. Nobody cares and they move on to what IS provable or working.

To waste years and dollars on trying to neutralize evidence that may undemine theories or reputations is not building science but defending opinions.

This is a sad turn toward political agendas and away from the purity of science.

As in all science, let facts do the defending, not words, not arguments. Evidence has always been the best argument for any claim. Defending unproven theories is not moving forward but freezing progress and beliefs.

If a scientific clan wants to argue with evidence, do it with evidence, not theories or declarations or rhetoric or accusations.

By adhering to this simple rule, fantastic momentum in any venture can be maintained.

RULE #3 - THE MOVING FORWARD RULE
Science should spend conspicuously more time building on what is true (proven) than trying to disprove evidence contradicting theories.

Alibrando's Rule #4 - The Weight of Evidence Rule
Favor the Weight of Evidence

FOR: Scientists & researchers (good rule for anyone)
BENEFICIARIES: Everyone with affection for common sense.

This rule is about common sense and honesty.

It applies to scientists, teacher, publishers, jurors and all of us making a decision based on the facts.

How many times have I learned a favorite theory from a professor or teacher and later found that there were other theories with possibly more evidence that I didn't even hear about?

Example:

Let's say there are twenty pieces of equal evidence. After reviewing all the twenty pieces of real evidence, not one but two theories emerge about what that evidence proves. The theories contradict each other. They cannot both be true. If eighteen pieces of evidence point one way and only two to the other theory, the one with greater evidence is more likely to be correct.

Why would anyone favor the theory with less evidence? Why would anyone say, "I know these two pieces of evidence are right but I don't quite understand those eighteen pieces of evidence."?

I am not talking about circumstantial evidence, but real evidence.

I could add weights to the evidence. If each EQUAL piece of evidence were put on a balance scale with A on the left side and B on the right. If there were two on A and eighteen on B, wouldn't the honest question be "We need to look more closely at the TWO EXCEPTIONS. Maybe they will support B after we review them more carefully.

Inversely, would it not be a suspicious declaration "We need to review those EIGHTEEN EXCEPTIONS that contradict the evidence of the two"?

When there is significantly more evidence to one theory than the other, the one with greater evidence is more likely to be correct.

If EVIDENCE presents itself and the weight shifts to the opposite theory it is abundantly clear the honest response would be to favor the theory with the weight of evidence.

Therefore, I present this as a rule for all honest analysts. Whether they are scientists, jurors, detectives, theologians, or any seeker of the truth:

RULE #4 - THE WEIGHT OF EVIDENCE RULE
Favor the Weight of Evidence

Alibrando's Rule #5 - The Cap Rule
If you can't prove a theory after spending enormous sums of money over many years, try another theory.

For: Those seeking funding and those granting funding.
BENEFICIARIES: Taxpayers, charitable donors, United States of America, all nations sharing scientific knowledge and research, the progression of science.

There should be a maximum limit on proving a theory; if failing at that limit, it should be categorized a false theory. Hey, we are talking about no evidence.

What seems to need regulation here are not the unpopular theories but the popular ones. If we invest in a failing business we are tempted to spend more on it in hopes of salvaging what we have invested.

A failed theory has an impact on a scientist's reputation, especially if a large sum of money has been invested. Sometimes there are even large networks of scientists and workers who support a flawed theory. Who wants failure? Nobody. Who wants to lose their reputation? Nobody. Who wants to lose funding? Nobody. We have a motive for wanting to continue a failed theory.

If the scientists can keep saying, "No, it's true, look at this new evidence." And the government guy or the rich donor says, "That's evidence?"

"Well, sure it is. Blah, blah, blah ... and of course it may be a little over your head but we all agree we are onto something."

"Duh, okay. You're the expert. Want more money?"

Reputations have been saved. The inevitable truth is delayed and the myth continues.

This rule's purpose is to cap the expense and stop only the ridiculous efforts and expense of trying to validate something that continues to be un-provable.

Sure, there are wealthy people that want to fund scientific quests for philosophical reasons. Go ahead. But governments (meaning taxpayers) shouldn't do this.

Since reputations are on the line and embarrassment is to be avoided, countless millions are spent on "popular" rather than scientific notions. The public should not have to fund such agendas. Nor should the public be subjected to false theories that should be considered EVEN MORE FALSE after spending large sums of money and still being unable to prove the theory/theories.

STOP. Think about it. The more time and money invested on a theory that continues to NOT show progress should not validate it. That theory should become less and less valid the more time and money that is spent unsuccessfully. It isn't working. It remains unproven.

Sadly, if an idea can overcome cynics and become popular, it is easier to get support for that idea. There is also the desire to not embarrass well-established figures in science with new evidence; evidence that can ruin the professional reputations of the revered "grandfathers" and many of their followers.

To do such a thing seems disrespectful and disloyal. But this is not supposed to be a community of people loyal to each other; this group is supposed to be feverishly loyal to the truth—that is genuine science. The bond between scientists should be this mutual uncompromising pursuit of pure science. It should not be a brotherhood of protecting each others' reputations with secret agendas contrary to science.

Consider the following as possible right now:

1. Scientists who present evidence contrary to the "Established Fathers" (those who are already getting funding) shall be tagged, ridiculed, blackballed and the public will be warned of their "unscientific" evidence by the "Established Fathers and followers."

2. Those in power (well funded "Established Fathers") will publicly discredit those presenting evidence challenging their established theories.

3. Those in power (well funded "Established Fathers") will hire and teach new scientists what they ought to pursue and what they ought to believe. The new underling scientists are warned against presenting any evidence contrary to what is maintained to be true, especially to the public. To challenge one's predecessor or teacher is disrespectful and will result in pulled funding.

4. By having immense authority in each respective scientific circle, the well funded "Established Fathers" gain acceptance that their expertise and reputation is more credible than evidence. Thus THEY (not evidence) dictate the "true" science.

I know it sounds a little cynical but in my life almost every time I am confused by illogical behavior, I have discovered some money motive behind the scenes.

The only way unproven theories can enjoy longevity in the mainstream of acceptance is:

1. Popularize it publicly, generate emotional excitement about possibilities, and create a demand for success.
2. Generate loyalty to the cause.
3. Make threats of no grant money to those disagreeing with theory.

Obviously, these are wrong and unethical. Therefore, here is my observation: If after so many dollars (you decide the amount) and so many years (you decide the time limit) of research without success (convincing EVIDENCE), the theory has piqued. Its season is over.

So here is the RULE: After ample time and money has been spent on theory research without proving the theory, it shall be officially certified by the scientific community as a failed theory and categorized as such: "A FAILED THEORY." Until such time as real evidence is provided it shall remain in that status.

RULE #5 - THE CAP RULE
If you can't prove a theory after spending enormous sums of money over many years, try another theory.

Alibrando's Rule #6 - The Exception Rule
An exception should never outweigh the norm in relevance.

FOR: Teachers and professors teaching students
BENEFICIARIES: students, the respect of logic, people who would prefer to argue about important things rather than outrageous claims.

To say something isn't true simply because there is a 1 in a million chance that there could be an exception is a ridiculous conclusion. That is far too much weight to give to an exception.

Any exception should be noted but should not be given the disproportionate weight to destroy a norm.

Examples:
1. We don't know of any cases where one species gives birth to another species but it is possible. We have seen some deformed frogs due to radiation exposure.
2. We have never created life in a laboratory but it is possible. Once we do it we will know that is definitely how all life began.
3. We have never seen anything of significance invented or constructed from hurricanes or earthquakes but it is

possible. Because we saw something like a box formed by some fence pieces back in 1952 after a storm.

To say evidence is inadequate because there is an exception may prove that it is not a 100% law. To say something is not true because a rare exception is possible is an effort to confuse the facts.

Example:
A defense lawyer points out that his client did shoot the man he was arguing with but it is possible that he didn't realize he had a gun in his hand pointed at the man. He tells the story of how something like this could actually happen.

Example:
Random accidents cause disrepair, dysfunction and destruction except possibly once in a million scenarios. In one scenario, maybe a leaning fence was straightened in a windstorm. Is this not ridiculous "proof" that the universe and all life were created this way? Shall we ignore the 999,999,999 evidences that hurricanes ruin property?

Shall we ignore the 999,999,999 evidences of things manufactured by mankind always require his intelligence and conscious intention?

Shall we ignore the evidence and allow a rare and very unlikely event to disproportionately skew our conclusion? No. It is ridiculous.

Here is a comical quest: The greatest scientific minds in the world, with a wealth of resources, try to create life in a laboratory to prove creating life requires no intelligence.

If they ever succeed, aren't they proving it does take great intelligence?

Those who practice embracing the exception as the norm and teach that the norm is invalid because of a rare exception may be entertaining, but they are hindering practical education. It is an escape from logic and deserves no respect, unless put in proper perspective.

Rule #6 - The Exception Rule
An exception should never outweigh the norm in relevance.

Alibrando's Rule #7 - The Fair Deduction Rule
To imply intelligence other than man is not to be rendered a religious or philosophical statement, as long as proper scientific methods are applied.

For: Anyone involved in the discussion of anything scientific.
Beneficiaries: Students, honest inquirers, and people too embarrassed to ask honest questions simply because they don't want to be accused of being religiously motivated.

Any correlation with or against religion is irrelevant in the pure pursuit of science.

All scientific points should be valued on their *scientific* merit regardless of fallout. The belief system the person speaking or writing may have is also irrelevant. Who cares if the person is an atheist if his conclusions can be proven true? Who cares if the person is Christian, Catholic, Mormon, Buddhist or Muslim? This is a weak, pitiful ploy of the media or any debater to overlook the *scientific* merit and focus the discussion on religious motives. It has NO place in a *scientific* discussion.

I suppose one primary question that this whole book is asking is, "What is the point of pretending there is no intelligence in the universe other than man, when the evidence is overwhelming?" Scientists can say "the wisdom of nature" or whatever they want to avoid mentioning God or aliens. However, it is flat dishonest and unscientific to state that there is conclusive knowledge proving there is no intelligence besides man. There is so little we know in light of all the knowledge that exists. To be so arrogant to state, "There is no intelligence behind all intelligent design except that which man himself has made," is far more a religious statement than a scientific one and disregards the evidence.

If you are a true scientist and want to avoid a religious discussion you can say honestly enough, "No comment," rather than "I know for a fact that it was all an accident" or "I know there is no intelligence behind the marvels of the universe."

How can any man claim to conclusively know all the secrets of the entire universe and call himself a scientist?

So the rule, that ought to be unnecessary, is necessary to restrain those who answer logical questions with a religious accusation instead of honest answers.

Rule #7 - The Fair Deduction Rule

To imply intelligence other than man is not to be rendered a religious or philosophical statement, as long as proper scientific methods are applied.

LAWS SUMMARY

Law #1 Original Beginnings
Un-provable Notion: Things originated gradually over billions of years.
Sensible Fact: Every species, started specifically with a very first one.
Technical Wording: *To exist, a thing must first begin, specifically.*

Law #2 Paired Origins
Un-provable Notion: A new male and female species emerges accidentally.
Sensible Fact: New species requiring male/female reproduction cannot continue without a new species mate.
Technical Wording: *All new species requiring two genders to reproduce must have both MALE and FEMALE emerge into existence at the same time, AND in the same location, AND with instinct and ability to reproduce.*

Law #3 Environmental Inventory
Un-provable Notion: AFTER a new species emerges they discover critical resources necessary and then evolve accordingly.
Sensible Fact: If you can't live in the environment, you die.
Technical Wording: *A newly emerged species must BEGIN compatible with the environment and already have all the necessary resources to survive.*

Law #4 Reproduction
Un-provable Notion: All species are descendents of not one, but many different species and classifications of species (mammal with reptile ancestors descended from fish, who descended from shellfish who are descendents of single-celled organisms).

SENSIBLE FACT: No species has babies that are a different species.
TECHNICAL WORDING: *No species is the origin of another species with a different number of chromosomes.*

LAW #5 EXTINCTION SCIENCE
UN-PROVABLE NOTION: Prehistoric, extinct species are all ancestors of modern creatures.
SENSIBLE FACT: When a creature becomes extinct it is gone, not evolving.
TECHNICAL WORDING: *The extinction of a species is not a species mutation.*

LAW #6 RANDOM RULE
UN-PROVABLE NOTION: Random, unintentional occurrences have accidentally designed everything on earth and in the universe that is not man-made.
SENSIBLE FACT: "Random" is contradictory to "designed."
TECHNICAL WORDING: *When something is random, it is not designed. When something is designed, it is not random.*

LAW #7 TIME & DETERIORATION
UN-PROVABLE NOTION: The more time given, the greater the likelihood of unsupervised organizing (removing flaws, improving capabilities) and expanding a larger, complex interdependent network.
SENSIBLE FACT: The longer anything goes without maintenance, the worse it gets.
TECHNICAL WORDING: *The more time needed to accomplish design accidentally, the greater the likelihood of failure.*

LAW #8 ORCHESTRATION
UN-PROVABLE NOTION: Things accidentally (or naturally) invent themselves to function and interact in a vast, interdependent network requiring no coordination.
SENSIBLE FACT: Coordinated interaction of independent systems requires skilled supervision.
TECHNICAL WORDING: *Integrating independent systems for a cause greater than their independent causes requires a perspective of all systems and the ability to coordinate them.*

Law #9 Order Requires Intelligence

Un-provable Notion: Designs in nature are not related to intelligence but rather results of many random accidents over billions of years.

Sensible Fact: It always takes brains to fix something, organize something new, or make something better.

Technical Wording: *Order and design are always an indication of intelligence.*

Ripple 1 of Law #9 Accidental Implausibility

Un-provable Notion: No matter how increasingly intelligent a design is, it can still happen billions of times by accident.

Sensible Fact: The more complex a design is, the less likely it is to be made by accident.

Technical Wording: *The likelihood of accidental occurrence decreases proportionately with the increase of order.*

Ripple 2 of Law #9 Deduced Intention

Un-provable Notion: Just because there is intelligent design, millions of flourishing species and an untold number of systems coordinated into a seamless, interdependent system doesn't mean it was done on purpose.

Sensible Fact: If a complex invention works, it was probably made to do it on purpose.

Technical Wording: *The likelihood of conscious, intelligent intention increases exponentially with an increase in order.*

Ripple 3 of Law #9 Intelligent Design

Un-provable Notion: Brilliant engineering does not require intelligence.

Sensible Fact: Working order is always evidence of intelligence.

Technical Wording: *Any functioning technology is proof of intelligence.*

Ripple 4 of Law #9 Proportional Intelligence

Un-provable Notion: The complexity of technology has no relation to intelligence.

Sensible Fact: The more complex an invention is, the smarter the inventor.

Technical Wording: *In proportion to the sophistication of the design, is the sophistication of the designer's intelligence.*

Law #10 Expert Opinion
Un-provable Notion: If you disagree with an expert you must be wrong.
Sensible Fact: An expert opinion is still an opinion.
Technical Wording: *An expert opinion is still an opinion, not fact.*

Ripple 1 of Law #10 Expert Fallibility
Un-provable Notion: Once a person has an impressive enough resume, he can no longer make mistakes related to his field of expertise.
Sensible Fact: No one is always right.
Technical Wording: *There is no college degree, profession or training that elevates a person to infallibility.*

Ripple 2 of Law #10 Consensus Myth
Un-provable Notion: Proof is required from amateurs but not necessarily from a group of experts.
Sensible Fact: Expert guesses, beliefs, opinions (whether 1 or 1,000) are still not facts unless proven.
Technical Wording: *Multiple expert opinions represent consensus, not fact.*

Ripple 3 of Law #10 Suspicious Resistance to Evidence
Un-provable Notion: Experts reject facts and evidence for good reasons.
Sensible Fact: Rejecting evidence can be ignorant, but when an expert does it, it is suspicious.
Technical Wording: *The more evidence an expert ignores, the more they prove they are against what is true.*

Law #11 Deference
Un-provable Notion: Man is the ultimate intelligence and there is no evidence that there is any intelligence greater than his.
Sensible Fact: We are students of nature.
Technical Wording: *When any technology is studied, it is the inferior learning from the superior.*

RULES SUMMARY

RULE #1 – THE SCIENTIFIC CONCLUSION RULE
No experiments, no proof—no conclusion.

RULE #2 – SCIENCE AND THEORY SEPARATION RULE
Science shall be clearly separated from theory.

RULE #3 – THE MOVING FORWARD RULE
Science should spend conspicuously more time building on what is true (proven) than trying to disprove evidence contradicting theories.

RULE #4 – THE WEIGHT OF EVIDENCE RULE
Favor the Weight of Evidence.

RULE #5 – THE CAP RULE
If you can't prove a theory after spending enormous sums of money over many years, try another theory.

RULE #6 – THE EXCEPTION RULE
An exception should never outweigh the norm in relevance.

RULE #7 – THE FAIR DEDUCTION RULE
To imply intelligence other than man is not to be rendered a religious or philosophical statement, as long as proper scientific methods are applied.

INVITATION

I am always more interested in the truth than defending any position. I also believe with years we always consider better ways of communicating some of the important concepts we want to express. Even though an idea may be 100% irrefutable, the wording may not be. In such a case, re-wording is needed and personally, I want it to still be easy enough for readers to understand.

I'm no expert and if I was I'd still know experts make mistakes and can keep learning.

I discussed this with the publisher, Tsaba House. Tsaba House has agreed to add any legitimate challenges or significantly improved statements in the next printing. If I have missed something obvious to you or maybe expressed more than one idea in a law or rule that should be expounded upon, let us know.

Here's your chance to become semi-published. We certainly cannot guarantee that your contribution or challenge will be printed, but we will promise it being reviewed and considered. Try not to be wordy in a philosophical way but as concise and logical as possible using the English language.

Send your challenges, improvements, enhancements (including pictures or graphs) or any other contributions to:

Tsaba House-NNST
2252 12th St.
Reedley, CA 93654
www.TsabaHouse.com
E-mail: info@TsabaHouse.com

INDEX

If you enjoyed this book and would like to pass one on to someone else or if you're interested in another Tsaba House title, please check with your local bookstore, online bookseller, or use this form:

Name_____

Address _____

City _____ State_____ Zip _____

Please send me:

_____ copies of *Nature Never Stops Talking* at $15.99 $ _____

_____ copies of *The Moody Pews* at $15.99 $ _____

_____ copies of *Streams of Mercy* at $15.99 $ _____

_____ copies of *The Payload* at $15.99 $ _____

_____ copies of *Your Rights to Riches* at $14.99 $ _____

_____ copies of *The Parenting Business* at $15.99 $ _____

California residents please add sales tax $ _____

Shipping*: $4.00 for the first copy and $2.00
for each additional copy $ _____

Total enclosed $ _____

Send order to:

Tsaba House
2252 12th Street
Reedley, CA 93654

or visit our website at www.TsabaHouse.com
or call (toll free) 1-866-TSABA-HS (1-866-872-2247)

For more than 5 copies, please contact the publisher for multiple copy rates.
*International shipping costs extra. If shipping to a destination outside the United States, please contact the publisher for rates to your location.